green

SNAKES
& OTHER REPTILES

. . . .

OF AUSTRALIA

Gerry Swan
Series Editor: Louise Egerton

NEW
HOLLAND

First published in Australia in 1998 by
New Holland Publishers (Australia) Pty Ltd
Sydney • London • Cape Town • Auckland
1/66 Gibbes Street Chatswood NSW 2067 Australia
218 Lake Road Northcote Auckland New Zealand
86 Edgware Road London W2 2EA United Kingdom
80 McKenzie Street Cape Town 8001 South Africa

Reprinted in 2000, 2001, 2002, 2004, 2005, 2006, 2008

National Library of Australia Cataloguing-in-Publication Data
     Swan, Gerry.
     Snakes and other reptiles of Australia.
     Includes index.

     ISBN 978-1-86436-342-5

     1. Reptiles — Australia. 2. Snakes — Australia — Identification.
     3. Reptiles — Australia — Identification. 4. Snakes — Australia — Identification.
     I. Title. (Series: Green guide).

     597.90994

Series Editor: Louise Egerton
Project Manager: Fiona Doig
Design and Cartography: Tricia McCallum
Picture Research: Bronwyn Rennex
Illustrations: Lawrence Lemmon-Warde
Reproduction: DNL Resources
Printed and bound by Everbest Printing Co., China

Photographic Acknowledgments
Abbreviations: NHIL = New Holland Image Library; LT = Lochman Transparencies; NF = Nature Focus.
Photographic positions: t = top, b = bottom, c = centre, m = main, i = inset, l = left, r = right, fc = front cover, bc = back cover, ff = front flap
Shaen Adey/NHIL: 4c, 21t, 27b, 42b, 50-51, 53t; **Eva Boogarrd/LT:** 13t, 40m, 52; **Clay Brice/LT:** 32b, 40i, 43b; **John Cann:** 14t, 51i, 55t, 57t, 72b; **R. Cook:** 13b, 31b, 35t, 63t, 65t, 88, 92m; **Harald Ehmann/Wildworks Australia:** 77t, 93i; **Pavel German:** fcm, ff, bct, contents, 11i, 19b, 20t, 23t, 29 c&b, 31t, 33b, 34i, 35b, 37, 38t, 47, 54t, 56, 58-59, 63b, 71t, 75b, 76t, 78b, 82b, 84t, 93m; **Phillip Griffin/LT:** 77b; **D. Green:** 91t; **A.E. Greer:** 70t; **P. Harlow:** 78t, 82t; **John Kleczkowski/LT:** 46b; **B. Lazell:** 9, 24b, 62, 65t, 66t, 67t; **Jiri Lochman/LT:** 6 t&b, 17t, 19t, 20b, 27t, 38b, 42t, 45i, 48, 54b, 55b, 57b, 59i, 73t, 75t, 80, 90,95c; **Marie Lochman/LT:** 86t; **Colin Limpus/NF:** 53b; **Peter Marsack/LT:** 81b; **Courtesy of Minolta:** 83; **Mike Prociv/Westro Pics:** 4t, 7b, 81t, 89i, 92i, 95i; **P.G. Roach/NF:** 32t; **Col Roberts/LT:** 46t, 49; **Gunther Schmida:** 4b, 7t, 10-11, 17b, 21b, 22, 24t, 25t, 28, 34m, 36m&i, 61t, 72t, 74, 86b, 87 t&b, 95b; **G. Shea:** 41; **Raoul Slater/LT:** 44-45; **Geoff Swan:** 18, 23b, 26, 29t, 30b, 33t, 4t, 60t, 67b, 68, 69t&b,70b, 7b, 73b, 79t, 84b, 89m, 91b; **Elizabeth Tasker:** 8b; **Mike Trenerry/Wetro Pics:** 12, 14b, 25b, 76b; **R. Valentic:** 8t, 15, 16, 30t, 39, 60b, 61b, 64t&b, 65b, 66b, 79b, 85t&b.

CONTENTS

An Introduction to Reptiles

❋

*R*eptiles really do seem to be the low life of the animal world. They never get good press and only feature when someone gets bitten by a snake or eaten by a crocodile. There is never a feature about how many rats and mice snakes kill. This book is intended for readers, both young and old, who do not know anything about reptiles but would like to find out about them. It is not intended to be a field or an identification guide — its purpose is to give the reader an insight into just how incredible these animals are.

Snakes are found in most habitats in Australia, from the desert to the alps.

Adaptability

When you consider that they are often regarded as some inferior 'cold-blooded' form of life, reptiles have adapted to an amazing extent. They occupy almost every habitat in all regions of Australia, from Mount Kosciuszko to the most arid inland areas. Certainly a variety of species can be found in inner city suburbs. Reptiles live in a diversity of environments: underground, on top of the ground, in trees and in rivers, lakes and oceans.

Both marine and freshwater turtles live a largely aquatic existence.

It is inevitable therefore that you will come into contact with reptiles. Perhaps in your own backyard, walking down the road or at a barbecue in the park or in the bush. Understanding them will make you feel more at ease. You do not have to like them but you should be able to tolerate and coexist with them. It is estimated that we kill over 5 million reptiles in Australia each year on our roads.

Lizards are well represented in Australia, especially in arid regions.

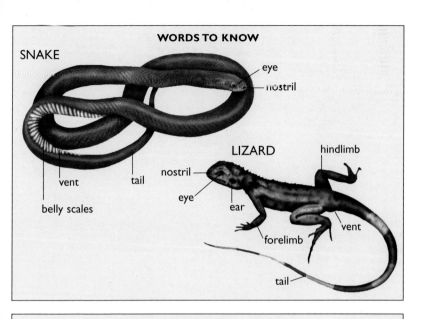

WORDS TO KNOW

SNAKE

eye
nostril
vent
tail
belly scales

LIZARD

hindlimb
nostril
eye
ear
forelimb
vent
tail

THE MAJOR REPTILE GROUPS

This table indicates the approximate number of species in each of the four major reptile groups found worldwide and in Australia.

Reptile Group	Type	Worldwide	Australia
Crocodiles		23	2
Turtles	Marine	8	6
	Freshwater	198+	17
Snakes	Blind	150	34
	Pythons	60	15
	File	3	2
	Colubrids	1600	11
	Elapids	180	81
	Sea snakes	50	31
	Sea kraits	6	2
Lizards	Geckos	900+	106
	Legless Lizards	36	34
	Goannas	34	26
	Dragons	325	65
	Skinks	1300+	363

Why is a Reptile's Skin Scaly?

Scales on the leg of a Freshwater Crocodile. These do not overlap as in many other reptiles.

*M*ost people know that snakes and lizards are reptiles. Turtles and crocodiles are also reptiles but not frogs, which are amphibians. Reptiles are vertebrates that breath air and depend on outside sources for body heat. The most obvious feature of reptiles is their non-porous, scaly skin. This helps to greatly reduce water loss from the body: as a result they do not need constant access to water. Some reptiles get all their liquid requirements from the prey they eat. This ability of reptiles to conserve body fluids means that they are able to inhabit very dry areas successfully.

ONE-LUNGED SNAKES
Most snakes have only one usable lung. A snake's hose-like body shape means the internal organs have to be elongated. Two lungs side by side do not really fit. Apart from pythons, which have two well-developed lungs, the left lung is reduced or absent in other snakes.

Why don't Reptiles need Regular Meals?

*U*nlike birds and mammals, reptiles do not need to maintain a constant body temperature, so they do not have to eat constantly. Being able to get by on an irregular supply of food means reptiles are able to occupy regions where food is not abundant.

A Stimson's Python subdues a mouse by coiling itself around the body and constricting it.

How Long do Reptiles Live?

*N*ot very much is known about the longevity of most reptile species in the wild but there is plenty of information on reptiles that have been kept in captivity. Certainly bluetongues, water dragons and other similarly sized lizards have been kept in captivity for between 20 and 30 years. The smaller species are not so long lived but some geckos have been kept for more than 10 years.

Snakes also are remarkably long lived in captivity and some have been kept for up to 20 years. In the wild they are unlikely to live as long. A less assured food supply, greater risk of predation and other hazards would reduce their life expectancy very significantly. Some species are known to only live for one or two years in the wild.

A curious feature of reptiles is that no matter how long they live, they continually replace their teeth. This is in contrast to mammals, which lose their teeth when they get old.

Shingleback Lizards like this one are thought to live for more than 20 years.

Setting Reptilian Records

*I*n Australia the Amethystine Python from northern Queensland has been recorded as exceeding 8 m and is our largest snake. The largest snake in the world is the Anaconda, which is reputed to reach 10 m. The largest Australian lizard is a goanna, the Perentie, which can reach 2.5 m in length. The largest lizard in the world is another goanna, the Komodo Dragon, from Indonesia, which can exceed 3 m in length.

An Amethystine Python waits for prey.

FOREVER GROWING

Did you know that some reptiles like pythons and crocodiles never stop growing? Their growth rate slows right down as they get older but in theory they can keep on growing into giants if they live long enough.

Are Reptiles Cold-blooded?

*R*eptiles are often referred to as 'cold-blooded' animals, which is an over simplification of a complex arrangement. Reptiles are ectotherms. This means that they rely on external heat sources to maintain a constant body temperature. Because they have no internal mechanisms to generate heat they must seek out warmth. Reptiles are therefore most numerous in tropical or hot arid areas where the air temperature is high and they do not have to spend a lot of time warming up. As they do not maintain a high body heat they require far less food than mammals or birds of similar size and so they have been able to successfully colonise areas that cannot sustain high numbers of birds and mammals.

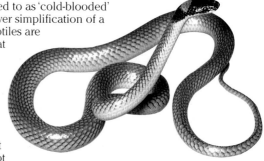

The shiny black head of the Red-naped Snake is a conspicuous feature.

BLACK HEADS
A surprising number of reptiles have black heads, even though the rest of their body is a light colour. It has been suggested that they can just poke their head out into the early morning sun without exposing the rest of their body to a possible attack while still cool and relatively slow. Heating up the head can quickly activate the brain and senses.

What Happens when the Temperature Drops?

*I*n tropical areas reptiles are active all year round but in temperate and cooler areas reptiles become inactive during the cold months and seek shelter in burrows, logs, under rocks and the like. They will remain there for several months and only emerge when the temperatures start to rise. The copperhead snake is exceptional. It is active at lower temperatures than any of the other large Australian snakes and has even been observed basking out in the sun during winter.

A copperhead snake, disturbed while basking in the sun.

How do Reptiles Keep Warm?

*A*fter the cool of the night reptiles have to warm up in the morning sun. This they do by basking until their body temperature is high enough to start their daily activities. Some reptiles flatten out to expose a greater body area to the heat and so warm up more quickly. In colder climates many reptiles have dark bodies allowing them to absorb greater heat than will a paler body. You may have seen lizards lying on bitumen roads, particularly in rural areas. The black surface absorbs heat from the sun and lizards flatten out on the road to absorb this heat a bit like an electric blanket.

During the day reptiles shuttle between sun and shade in order to keep their temperature at the desired level. If it gets too hot, they will disappear into shelter. Nocturnal reptiles can operate at lower temperatures. Some of these will actually heat up under cover by selecting sheltered spots that get the afternoon sun.

A male Nobbi Dragon takes advantage of a stump to warm itself up.

CAN REPTILES OVERHEAT?

Reptiles cannot just keep heating up. They reach a critical point where the temperature becomes lethal. The point at which this does become lethal varies between species but it can exceed 40°C. If the reptile cannot reduce its body temperature, it will very quickly die. This then is their problem: they need heat to raise their temperature and carry out normal daily activities and they must keep warm to be able to digest their food — this is particularly so with snakes — but too much heat will kill them.

SNAKES

Are all Snakes Venomous?

*N*ot all snakes are venomous and indeed most venomous snakes are not dangerous. There are far more non-venomous snakes than venomous ones worldwide but in Australia the opposite is the case and the majority are venomous. Unfortunately unless you are familiar with snakes it is not possible merely by looking to tell if a snake is venomous or not. Sometimes even the experts get confused.

> **AUSSIE SNAKES**
> Out of 11 families of snakes world-wide, seven are found in Australia and its surrounding coastal waters. They range in size from the tiny Flowerpot Snake, at only 12 cm long, to the massive Amethystine Python which can grow to 8.5 m. In this book average lengths are listed near the headings.

Which Snakes are Non-venomous?

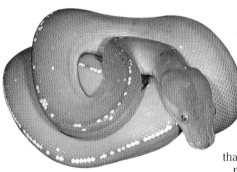

The beautiful Green Python is a non-venomous inhabitant of some rainforests in northern Queensland.

*I*n Australia, four of our seven families are regarded as non-venomous: the blind snakes, the pythons, the file snakes and the colubrids.

Non-venomous Families

The blind snakes have small shiny worm-like bodies with blunt heads and short tails that end in a spine. Their eyes are reduced to dark spots and the scales are a uniform size around the body (with none enlarged on the belly as in some other snakes). When handled, they have a tendency to emit a strong, pungent odour.

Pythons are muscular, usually heavily built and slow-moving. Most Australian pythons have heat-sensing pits in some of the scales of their lips. They all have 30 or more scale rows around the middle of the body and their belly scales are larger than the others. All pythons possess spurs (which are the vestiges of ancestral hindlimbs) on either side of their vent.

The file snakes are totally aquatic and have large robust bodies with a 'baggy' skin. Unlike the paddle-like tail of the typical sea snakes, the tails of the file snakes are narrow and can grasp things, so they are useful 'anchors'. The scales are small, very rough and rasp-like.

The colubrids are found across northern Australia and down the east coast. These snakes may be completely non-venomous, although some have enlarged, grooved, poison-conducting fangs at the back of the mouth but even these are not regarded as dangerous.

Which Snakes are Venomous?

Egg-eating Turtle-headed Sea Snakes foraging around coral reefs. Most sea snakes are highly venomous.

There are three venomous snake families in Australia: the elapids, the sea snakes and the sea kraits. All the elapid snakes are venomous, although most are only mildly so and are not considered to be dangerous. They all have fixed hollow fangs in the front of the upper jaw, connected on each side by a duct to the venom gland. There are 15–23 scale rows around the mid-body, excluding the broad belly scales.

The completely aquatic sea snakes have vertically compressed, paddle-shaped tails and nostrils which are situated on the top of the snout with flaps that close when the snake is submerged. The vast majority of sea snakes are very venomous but they are rarely encountered.

The Golden-crowned Snake is a non-dangerous elapid.

While essentially marine snakes, the sea kraits do come on to land, particularly to lay their eggs. All are characterised by numerous black cross-bands and laterally placed nostrils. Although very poisonous, sea kraits are reluctant to bite and are rarely encountered.

BITE WITHOUT VENOM

Did you know that when a venomous snake bites, it does not automatically mean the victim has been injected with venom? When biting defensively it may not inject any venom. That is why hospital staff will always wait to see if there are any signs of envenomation before they actually treat a bite.

What is Venom?

Venom is a modified saliva and it is only a relatively recent development in snake evolution. Saliva contains various enzymes that help to break down food for faster digestion — an important feature for reptiles. Some of these enzymes would be mildly toxic and over a long period of time, in some snake groups, this mildly toxic saliva has evolved to become a potent complex venom.

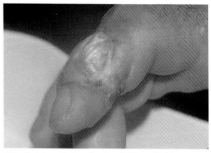

The flesh has died at the site of this snake bite.

Why do Snakes have Forked Tongues?

The forked tongue of a snake is not used in biting. It is a highly developed taste organ that is flicked in and out to pick up particles in the air. It is forked so that the snake can tell if the prey that it is tracking is to one side or the other of its body: whichever fork picks up the stronger scent is the one it will follow. Some people think snakes have a sting at the end of their tail. This is not the case, although the slight hook at the end of a blind snake's tail, which is an aid to burrowing, is also sometimes mistaken for a sting.

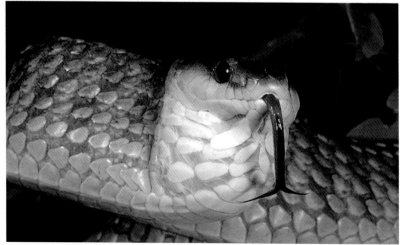

A Green Tree Snake with its tongue extended and the two forks widely separated, tasting the air for scent.

How Can I Recognise a Venomous Snake?

*T*here is no absolute method of telling a venomous snake from a non-venomous snake but it is certainly a good idea to know which dangerous snakes can be found in your area. Take the time to look at photographs in an appropriate field guide so you can identify your local dangerous snakes. Some can be readily identified because of their body form and size but colour alone is an extremely unreliable guide to identification as there is a great deal of variation in colour within many species.

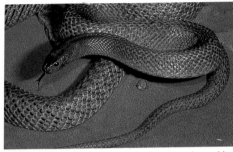

Although it is the most venomous land snake in the world, the Inland Taipan is an inoffensive, secretive snake.

It is worth remembering that although 70 per cent of Australian land snakes are venomous only about 20 per cent are regarded as being dangerously venomous. In Australia less than five people die from snake bites each year, despite it being the country with the most venomous snakes in the world. There are several reasons for this. One is that our snakes have short fangs. Another is that many inhabit remote areas where few people live. Added to this, Australia has very good medical facilities.

THE WORLD'S MOST VENOMOUS SNAKES

The snakes with the most toxic venom in the world are set out below. Those in italics are not Australian species. This rating is based on each species producing the same amount of venom but not all these snakes do produce the same amount. In fact some of the overseas snakes inject large amounts of venom and represent as great, if not greater, risk to human life than many Australian species.

1. Inland Taipan
2. Eastern Brown Snake
3. Taipan
4. Eastern Tiger Snake
5. Reevesby Island Tiger Snake
6. WA Tiger Snake
7. Chappell Island Tiger Snake
8. Death Adder
9. Western Brown Snake
10. Copperhead
11. *Indian Cobra*
12. Dugite
13. Papuan Black Snake
14. Stephen's Banded Snake
15. Rough-scaled Snake
16. *King Cobra*
17. Blue-bellied Black Snake
18. Collett's Snake
19. Mulga Snake
20. Red-bellied Black Snake
21. Small-eyed Snake
22. *Eastern Diamond Back Rattlesnake*

Pythons

50cm–5m

Like most pythons, the Olive Python is nocturnal. Growing up to 6 m, it can subdue very large prey.

Pythons occur in all mainland Australian States but they are most common in the tropical north where eight of Australia's 15 species are found. They range from the Pygmy Python, with a total length of 50 cm, to the largest snake in Australia, the Amethystine Python, recorded at 8.5 m long. All except the Woma and the Black-headed Python have a broad head, a relatively narrow neck and heat-sensitive pits on their lips.

The pits are capable of detecting differences in temperature and assist in locating warm-blooded prey: all pythons constrict their prey. They are mainly nocturnal but they are sometimes encountered basking during the day. Although pythons are non-venomous, they have sharp backward-curving teeth and can inflict a painful bite. Pythons are the only snakes to retain the vestiges of hindlimbs: these take the form of spurs situated on either side of their vent.

Broody Pythons

All pythons lay eggs. The female pushes them into a mound that she can coil around while they incubate. She will stay coiled around the eggs, not eating, and leaving only to heat up in the sun. When the young emerge from the eggs and disperse the female departs to find food for herself. From birth the hatchlings are on their own and must fend for themselves.

> **A RECENT DISCOVERY**
>
> The Oenpelli Python was only 'discovered' in the 1970s, although it was well known to local Aboriginal communities. This python is known to reach 4 m and possibly much bigger. A slender snake with a long grasping tail, it inhabits only the cliffs and gorges of Arnhem Land in the Northern Territory.

Being big and brown, the Woma is sometimes mistaken for a venomous brown snake and consequently killed.

Woma Python 2.5m

Pythons generally constrict their prey by coiling around it and increasing the pressure every time the animal breathes out. The prey then suffocates as it cannot draw another breath. The Woma or Sand Python has a different strategy. It locates much of its prey down burrows where there is not enough room to coil and constrict. Instead the Woma squashes the victim against the burrow wall with its body. Womas may often be found with scarring on their bodies where the victim did not give in quietly.

These pythons are also known to lure prey by wriggling the end of their tails in much the same way as death adders. As a consequence, adults of this species may be found with part of their tails damaged or missing, where a curious bird, mammal or reptile has had a snap before being attacked itself.

Water Python 3m

The Water Python is a northern Australian species that, as its name suggests, is usually associated with water. It is found around freshwater billabongs, watercourses, lagoons and swamps and feeds on mammals, birds, particularly waterbirds, and reptiles. It is also known to eat birds' eggs.

The Water Pythons around Fogg Dam near Darwin have been found to occur in huge numbers. Their biology is tied in to that of the water

The Water Python is another of the large Australian pythons found in many areas across northern Australia.

rat, which is also abundant there. The only food in sufficient quantity for newly hatched Water Pythons to eat are baby water rats. If the rats fail to breed or breed too early, then only very few baby pythons will survive from that year.

Carpet Pythons

2–3m

The black and yellow patterning of the Diamond Python provides effective camouflage in the trees.

Carpet pythons are the most widespread group of pythons in Australia, occurring across much of the mainland. Robust snakes, they may vary considerably in colour and form. The carpet pythons from the rainforests of northeastern Queensland can be a striking black or dark brown with long bold yellow stripes or blotches. The so-called Diamond Python that occurs along the east coast from northern New South Wales to Victoria is the one encountered by many people: olive black with creamy yellow rosettes along the body. Other variations occur in inland, northern and western Australia.

Carpet pythons are generally ambush predators rather than active hunters. They select a spot next to a trail used by other animals and lie in wait.

RAT-CATCHERS
Carpet pythons were frequently used in warehouses to keep down rats and mice. They were reckoned to be better than cats because they could get into places where nests were located and eat all the young rodents as well.

Mating and Mothering Diamond Pythons

During spring female Diamond Pythons lay down a scent trail as they move around and males pick this up and follow it. The snakes form groups of one or two females and several males. The males all attempt to mate with the females and the strongest sperm from each male will fertilise the eggs. Consequently the hatchlings will have the same mother but very possibly different fathers.

Female carpet pythons are known to 'shiver' as they coil themselves around their incubating eggs. This muscle contraction raises the mother's body temperature, helping to maintain a high temperature for the incubating eggs.

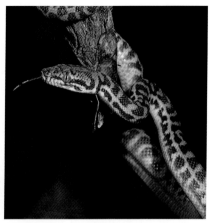

Children's pythons are efficient hunters of small animals, particularly bats.

Children's Pythons 50cm–1m

Children's python is a name applied to a group of three small pythons. Contrary to popular belief their name does not signify that they are pythons for children; it is in fact the name of an English naturalist, J.G. Children after whom the snakes were named. They are, however, popular snakes with reptile keepers and are a good species for young people to keep because of their small size and placid temperament.

Children's pythons occur over much of Australia and are often associated with rock outcrops and caves where they are very adept at catching bats. They will climb a rock face at the entrance to a cave where bats are roosting and wait there until the bats fly out in the evening. They will catch a bat flying past and eat it hanging in mid-air, secured to the rocks only by their tails. They also eat frogs, lizards and rodents.

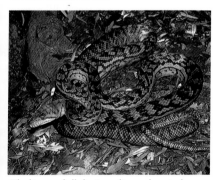

The biggest of all the Australian pythons is the Amethystine Python, which reaches a massive 5 m.

Amethystine Python 5m

The Amethystine Python, which is also known as the Scrub Python, is Australia's largest snake. Specimens have been measured at more than 8.5 m in length but this is quite exceptional and a 5 m snake is regarded as very big.

The name of this species comes from the milky iridescent sheen on its scales, which gives it an amethyst-like colour. Unlike many of the very big boas from overseas, this snake has a slim body. Just the same it can eat large prey and will kill and eat wallabies and bush pigs. More often it takes birds, fruit bats, possums and similar sized mammals. It is usually active at night and younger animals are mainly tree dwelling. The large adults are more terrestrial but they are still quite capable of getting up into the trees. Male Amethystine Pythons are aggressive with one another during the mating season and at such times they will engage in combat.

How do Snakes Move?

With up to 400 vertebrae, snakes have remarkable flexibility and some can travel at up to 10 kph. There are four different ways in which they may move. The usual method is an undulating movement in which the snake uses irregularities on the ground to get leverage and push its body against them. Done at a number of points along the body at the same time, this creates a constant undulating flow. Brown snakes and whipsnakes move like this.

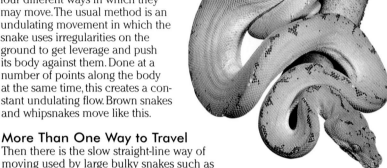

More Than One Way to Travel

Then there is the slow straight-line way of moving used by large bulky snakes such as pythons. The head and forebody are stretched straight forward. The belly scales then gain a hold and the snake advances by contracting its body muscles and dragging the rest of itself forward.

The Green Tree Python spends a lot of time coiled in trees, waiting for prey.

In the concertina method sometimes adopted by Brown Tree Snakes the snake forms a series of body loops and then pushes its head and forebody forward. Having obtained a purchase, it draws the body loops forward and the process is repeated.

Sidewinding is a means of locomotion used in soft sand or mud whereby a snake moves diagonally along a surface. The White-bellied Mangrove Snake, for example, sometimes moves by sidewinding. It pushes its head and neck against a surface and flicks its body forward in a loop. Once the tail and back part of the body gain a grip, it flicks its body forward in a loop again.

The Keelback Snake swims with the same undulating movement it uses on land.

How do Crocodiles and Turtles Move on Land?

*C*rocodiles are essentially aquatic and they are strong swimmers that use their tails to propel themselves. They usually slide along the ground but they can walk slowly with their bodies raised off the ground. Freshwater Crocodiles can actually gallop over short distances and are reputed to reach speeds of up to 18 kph.

A Green Turtle resting after laying her eggs on Heron Island.

Marine turtles are extremely awkward on land as their limbs are really flippers. In the ocean, however, they are able to 'fly' through the water using these limbs. Freshwater turtles have limbs that are clawed and webbed. They can move quickly enough on land and in the water they can swim extremely well.

How do Other Reptiles Move?

*T*he majority of lizards have four limbs and in many, such as dragons and goannas, these are well developed so they can move around quickly. The Sand Goanna and the Frilled Lizard can even run on only their hindlegs. Those with less well-developed limbs, such as bluetongues, can only slide along the ground, pushing themselves with their short legs.

Reptiles that live underground, like the sand sliders and worm skinks, make their way through the sandy soil using their snouts as shovels. Most of these have highly polished scales. The blind snakes have points on the ends of their tails which they can use to get a firm grasp and push themselves forward. Still other lizards literally slide through the top layer of soil or even 'swim' through sand.

SWIMMING SNAKES

All snakes can swim, even those found in desert areas, and all land snakes will take to water occasionally. Tiger snakes in South Australia have been seen swimming in the ocean several kilometres from the nearest land. It is believed they were moving between islands. Of course sea snakes and the aquatic colubrids swim very well and many have tails that are vertically compressed to assist.

Rising up onto its hindlegs a Sand Goanna can present a formidable appearance to an enemy.

File Snakes

70cm–2m

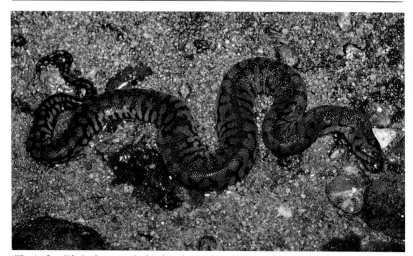

The Arafura File Snake is completely adapted to a life in the water and cannot cope with being on land.

*F*ile snakes are bizarre-looking reptiles. Totally aquatic, they have a very baggy, loose-fitting skin, which is coarse and file-like to the touch. This baggy skin flattens out when they are swimming, allowing the snake to move efficiently through the water. They also have nostrils that are high on the snout and have valves that close when the snake is under water. Out of the water they have trouble moving around and are almost completely helpless.

Two file snakes are found in Australia: the Arafura File Snake (see map), which occurs in freshwater creeks and billabongs, and the Little File Snake, which is found in coastal waters such as estuaries. Neither is venomous.

Rough Skin: Handy Grip

File snakes have a grasping tail for gripping roots or snags in the water to prevent them from being carried about by the current. They eat fish, which they squeeze to death. Their rough skin is very useful when holding this slippery prey, giving the snake a good grip as it constricts the fish prior to eating it.

The Arafura File Snake is a favourite food of local Aboriginal people, who get into the billabongs and stand often waist-deep to feel about with their feet for the snakes beneath the banks and logs. Female file snakes may only reproduce about every 8–10 years because they need to build up reserves of energy to develop their young. Because they are slow moving and not very good at catching fish, it may take several years to accumulate sufficient energy.

The eyes of blind snakes distinguish little more than light and dark.

Blind Snakes   10–75cm

The blind snakes, or worm snakes as they are sometimes called, are harmless snakes with highly polished, worm-like bodies and closely fitting scales. They eat the eggs and larvae of ants and termites and their bodies are designed to get into these animals' nests without being eaten themselves. The smooth skin leaves no room for ants or termites to take hold and each species knows what size nest to enter: small blind snakes do not go into bulldog ant nests, for example, as these ants are large enough to attack and kill them. The larger blind snakes can however go into such nests without a problem.

Some blind snakes give off an unpleasant odour when handled and this is thought to be some form of anti-predator deterrent.

Blind snakes are found over much of mainland Australia. They live underground most of the time but occasionally they are found above ground at night.

A Brown Tree Snake in a strike position.

Colubrids   1–2m

In most places in the world the colubrids are the most widespread and common of the snakes but in Australia this is not the case because they arrived here after the elapids. They have only become established in northern Australia, although the distribution of a few extends down the east coast. Only two, the Green Tree Snake and Brown Tree Snake, are found as far south as Sydney.

Many colubrids are found in or near water. They are divided into two groups: the non-venomous group and the back-fanged venomous group, which have enlarged, grooved poison-conducting fangs at the backs of their mouths that are capable of injecting venom. None of these Australian back-fanged snakes are regarded as dangerous but they can — and do — bite.

CRAB-EATING SNAKE

One of the venomous colubrid snakes, the White-bellied Mangrove Snake, is a crab eater. It pins the crab down and eats it whole or, if the crab is too big, it pulls off its legs and claws first. The White-bellied Mangrove Snake is the only snake known to dismember prey before eating it.

Where do Reptiles Live?

The Adelaide Pygmy Bluetongue Lizard lives in abandoned spider burrows from where it pounces on passing insects.

HOT AND COLD REPTILES

The arid areas of Australia support a very high diversity of reptiles, with over 40 species in some locations. By each species specialising in diet, activity times and shelter sites, competition between them can be minimised.

At the other end of the scale, a few lizards and snakes actually live above the winter snowline. The White-lipped Snake and the Alpine Water Skink hibernate beneath the snow and re-emerge when the snow melts. They have adapted to living in a cool climate and making the most of the shorter warm season.

Reptiles are a very versatile lot. There are probably very few places in Australia where at least one or two reptiles cannot be found. Some, such as the Wall Lizard and Garden Skink, even occur in inner city suburbs. Most reptiles live on the ground; they are known as terrestrial reptiles. Within this terrestrial environment there are many different niches. Some of the legless lizards and the comb-eared skinks live in grass clumps, others, such as the Gidgee and Cunningham's Skinks and many goannas, use rock crevices and outcrops and still others, like the Fat-tailed Gecko and the Adelaide Pygmy Bluetongue, live in spider burrows.

When is it Useful to be Limbless?

Limbs are nothing but a bother if you are a burrower. Many snakes (which are, of course, limbless) are burrowers that spend most of their lives under the ground. Burrowers are said to be fossorial. These snakes have shiny body scales and the scales on the head tend to be hard and shaped for burrowing.

Perhaps surprisingly, many lizards have adopted a similar way of living. Many have either tiny limbs, only two limbs or none at all. Inhabiting the area just below the surface, they benefit from the sun warming the ground surface and litter while being protected from predators. When the temperature gets too high they move down into deeper, cooler soil.

Legless lizards evolved a snake-like lifestyle.

Do any Snakes and Lizards Live in Water?

Macleay's Water Snake inhabits freshwater waterways.

Sea snakes and file snakes are truly aquatic and live their whole lives in the water, even being born there. Several of the colubrid snakes, such as Macleay's Water Snake and the mangrove snakes, live in fresh water or in mangrove swamps. A number of other snakes and lizards, like the Red-bellied Black Snake that feeds on frogs and the Water Dragon and Water Skink that eat insects, prefer to be around water but they are not truly aquatic.

What do Termite Mounds Offer Reptiles?

Quite a few reptiles use termite mounds extensively. Several geckos and skinks shelter in the galleries of giant mounds and no doubt feed on the inhabitants. Such mounds make a secure home for the Pygmy Python which, in turn, feeds on these lizards. Several goannas dig holes in termite mounds and lay their eggs deep inside; here they are sealed in by termites and kept at a suitable temperature.

Do Reptiles Inhabit Trees?

Many reptiles inhabit trees some, most or all of their time; these animals are known as arboreal reptiles. Many of the geckos are tree-dwellers, and so are some of the skinks. Some of the dragons and goannas have also taken to spending most of their time off the ground. The rainforest dragons come down to lay their eggs but otherwise they are rarely seen out of the trees. Several snakes, such as the Pale-headed Snake, are thought to be almost entirely arboreal, catching their food of lizards and frogs up in the trees.

Boyd's Forest Dragon prefers to live in trees.

How Can I Find Reptiles?

*R*eptiles are protected in Australia and it is illegal to disturb them in any way. You should make yourself familiar with what you can and cannot do, and make sure you are acting within the regulations of your State.

To find reptiles keep your eyes and ears open, and move slowly and quietly. Study the area ahead looking out for animals. In rocky areas, examine crevices and ledges. Stop when you see or hear a reptile. If you are lucky it may not have seen you or you may still be far enough away for it not to flee. Only experience will tell you how close you can get to a particular species before it will run away.

Why Can't I Find Any Reptiles?

*A*lthough occurring in all regions, reptiles are not highly visible like birds. They tend to be more secretive and a high proportion of species live under the ground or are nocturnal. Finding a particular species depends very much on the weather conditions, the time of year and time of day. Except in the tropical north, most reptiles become dormant during winter. Spring and early summer are the best times to see reptiles as many species are actively seeking mates and foraging for food.

Usually the more hours you spend looking, the more chance you have of seeing something. Do not be disappointed if the first time you see little or nothing. Keep at it. Returning to the same locality at different times of the year in different weather conditions will yield species not seen previously.

The Southern Leaf-tailed Gecko has a shape and colour that makes it hard to see in its natural habitat.

Where do Reptiles Hide?

A Mulga Snake emerges from its hiding place among rocks. Snakes can get into very tight crevices.

You are likely to see more lizards than snakes since they are more numerous and many are active during the day. They are also more visible. Those that are not seen in the open must be searched for beneath close-fitting objects on the ground, such as rocks, logs, sheets of tin, timber and the like. Always carefully replace any material lifted and keep disturbance to a minimum.

In cooler weather some reptiles will retreat down burrows or into the surface layers of soil. Larger reptiles can often be identified by observation but most smaller species require close scrutiny or even capture to identify positively.

Caught in the Spotlight

Spotlighting on roads at night can be very rewarding. Many reptiles are nocturnal and seek out roads because of the warmth they retain or they may be simply crossing the road during normal foraging activities. You need to choose a road that does not have much traffic with extensive areas of bush. Driving slowly (5–10 km) along these roads in the right conditions can reveal a variety of reptiles.

BEWARE THE HOLLOW LOG

Hollow logs are a favourite hiding spot for lizards and snakes as well as other animals. For this reason they should not be chopped open or burnt. By sitting quietly near a log you may see a lizard emerge to bask in the sun. A snake is more likely to stay hidden within. Never put your hand into a hollow log as you may possibly pull it out with a snake or spider attached to it.

Reptiles can sometimes be caught in the glare of car headlights as they soak up the warmth of a road after a hot day.

Which is the Biggest Australian Snake Family?

A Death Adder from the Barkly Tableland in Queensland. This species is among the dangerous venomous snakes and one of the few that does not move away but remains motionless and hidden when approached.

The elapid family is the major group of land snakes in Australia. Out of a total of 143 species of snakes known to live here, 81 are elapids so they account for 70 per cent of our snake fauna. When you consider that there are about 180 elapid species worldwide, Australia certainly has its fair share.

Elapids are all venomous snakes. They have fixed, hollow fangs at the front of their upper jaw, which are connected to venom glands behind the eye. Because each fang is fixed it is relatively short, unlike the overseas vipers where the fangs are much longer but they can fold up against the top of the mouth.

Are All Venom-carriers Dangerous?

Some are dangerous, most are not. Only about 20 elapids in Australia would be regarded as being dangerous. While most of the non-dangerous ones can bite, they would cause a reaction similar to a bee or wasp sting, or possibly no reaction at all.

Many elapids are small, less than 60 cm long, with the smallest being only 30 cm long. A considerable number are nocturnal or burrowers and therefore rarely seen. The really dangerous snakes are the large elapids, which tend to be the ones most commonly encountered.

Elapid snakes are found throughout Australia. Diversity varies: while there are as few as three species in Tasmania, there are more than 20 species in north-eastern Queensland. Some are specialised in their requirements but many are generalists and may occupy a wide range of environments: provided there is food and shelter, they will be there.

Why Do Snakes Come around Houses?

A snake makes itself at home.

*T*he larger elapid snakes eat a lot of mice and rats, and in doing so they play a significant role in keeping down the numbers of some of these pests. This is one reason why larger snakes are found around houses and outbuildings: they are attracted by the various rodents that live there.

The small elapids are mainly lizard and frog eaters but several, like the shovel-nosed snakes, eat the eggs of other reptiles. The frog eaters may be attracted to the frogs found in suburban fish ponds.

Some snakes may wander into backyards in search of a mate. Others are drawn in by very hot weather to seek the cool shelter found in or under houses.

Do Small Snakes Specialise in Certain Foods?

*T*he Golden-crowned Snake, White-crowned Snake and Dwarf-crowned Snake are three small species that are entirely nocturnal and feed mainly on small skinks. These are found while they are inactive in overnight shelters. The Golden-crowned Snake often seems to just eat the lizards' tails. Whether this is accidental, the snake grabbing the wrong end, or deliberate because the lizard will grow another tail, only the snake knows.

The smallest of the elapids is the Black-striped Snake, which only grows to 30 cm in length. It has a very restricted distribution occurring near Perth in Western Australia. This snake feeds on small burrowing lizards, which it stalks beneath the surface until it is within striking distance. It then emerges from the sand and strikes downwards onto its prey.

Golden-crowned Snake in defence pose; these snakes are often attacked and killed by domestic cats.

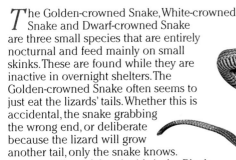

The Bandy Bandy's defensive display: it arches its body into a large raised loop.

CHOOSY EATERS

The unmistakable Bandy Bandy eats blind snakes almost exclusively. It locates them underground where the blind snakes dine on termite and ant eggs. One meal probably goes a long way because a Bandy Bandy can eat a blind snake as long as itself.

A Yellow-faced Whipsnake outside its rocky retreat.

Whipsnakes 50–180cm

One of the more obvious groups of medium-sized elapid snakes are the six species of whipsnakes. These snakes are slender, fast-moving and active during the day. Their scales are smooth but not glossy. They have large eyes on which they rely a great deal because the bulk of their diet consists of lizards that are active during the daytime.

Whipsnakes make up a widespread group. The largest is the Greater Black Whipsnake, also known as the Papuan Whipsnake, which occurs in northern areas of Australia. The only whipsnake to occur outside Australia, it is also found in New Guinea. The most commonly encountered whipsnake is the Yellow-faced Whipsnake, recognisable by a distinctive 'comma' around the eye. Whipsnakes are egg-layers and the Yellow-faced Whipsnake is known to make use of communal nests: in Queensland more than 600 eggs were found under one rock slab, the clutches of perhaps 75 females. The reason why some reptiles do this is uncertain.

The dark colour on a young Curl Snake's head will fade.

Curl Snake 60cm

The Curl Snake is a widespread species over much of central and eastern Australia and it occurs in a wide range of habitats. It has a robust body that may be almost any shade of brown or red-brown and a broad flat head. A nocturnal snake, it feeds mainly on small lizards and mammals. A live-bearer, it produces 2–6 young in spring.

The name of this snake refers to the defensive posture it adopts when alarmed. It will curl its body into a series of coils and strike out from this position. The bite of a large specimen should be regarded as potentially lethal.

It has been suggested that there are actually several species of curl snake. In some northern populations the snakes grow larger than the more southerly groups and these have a significantly higher venom yield. There are conflicting accounts of the symptoms of Curl Snake bites. Some reports state that its bite is extremely painful; others maintain that there is only local pain and swelling.

The cold-adapted White-lipped Snake.

Southern Snakes 40–60cm

The southern snakes are a group of elapids that seem to prefer the cooler climates. All four species belong to the genus *Drysdalia* and occur throughout southern Australia including Tasmania. One of them, the White-lipped Snake (see map), is the most cold-adapted of all our snakes and occurs above the winter snowline at Mount Kosciuszko.

As would be expected for snakes preferring the cooler regions, these are all live-bearers. The White-lipped Snake breeds every 2–3 years in Tasmania but it is an annual breeder elsewhere. The juveniles of all species have brightly coloured bellies ranging from yellow through orange to red. This coloration becomes more subdued as the snake matures. This may be an anti-preda-tion device as juvenile White-lipped Snakes have been observed to roll onto their backs and into a knot thereby displaying their colourful bellies. While venomous, they are small snakes with short fangs and are considered unlikely to cause any concern.

The Stephen's Banded Snake lives in trees.

Venomous Tree Snakes 60cm

This is an unusual group of snakes com-prising three species all belonging to the genus *Hoplocephalus;* the Broad-headed Snake, the Pale-headed Snake and the Stephen's Banded Snake. These medium-sized snakes are all nocturnal and tree- or rock-dwelling. To assist them in climbing trees, they have keeled scales on their belly.

All three species are inhabitants of the east coast and live in forested areas. They are easily aroused if disturbed and have a potent venom that can cause serious illness. Females breed every second or third year rather than each year.

The Broad-headed Snake has an interesting annual cycle. It spends the winter months under thin sandstone rocks or in crevices on the edge of sand-stone escarpments. In the hotter weather it moves to the upper hollow limbs of large eucalypts and stays there until autumn. Unfortunately 200 years of removing bush rock for Sydney suburban gardens has rendered this snake now extremely vulnerable. The Pale-headed Snake is considered to be almost completely arboreal, rarely being seen on the ground Stephen's Banded Snake, while spending a lot of time on trees is also found in rock outcrops where it utilises the deep crevices for shelter.

How does Snake Venom Work?

The fangs of this venomous snake are clearly visible.

Snake venom has three main functions: firstly to incapacitate prey so that the snake can subdue and eat it; secondly to aid digestion of the prey by breaking down the tissue; and thirdly, as a deterrent to possible predators.

Venom is not a single substance but rather it is a mixture of components; it is actually a modified saliva. The venom is stored in glands situated behind the eyes and it is carried to the front of the head where it enters a duct or groove in the fangs and travels down to the tip. A snake can control the amount of venom that is delivered to the fangs. When biting a person, a snake frequently injects no venom at all.

What does Venom Do?

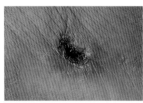

The site of a Tiger Snake bite after seven days have elapsed.

There are three general categories of toxins in snake venom. There are neurotoxins, which affect the nerve functions, especially the heart and lung muscles. This causes paralysis of the diaphragm muscles and suffocation. Then there are myotoxins, which damage muscles and break down muscle fibre. The last category is the haemotoxins. These affect the blood and interfere with the clotting properties of blood. Some haemotoxins are coagulants, which cause small blood clots to form in the veins; others are anticoagulants, which prevent clotting and cause bleeding and haemorrhages. Haemotoxins also contain components that destroy red blood cells.

What are the Symptoms of a Snake Bite?

The symptoms of a snake bite vary considerably depending on the species but common symptoms are headache, drowsiness, sweating and nausea. The lymph nodes in the armpits and groin may become painful and swollen. As the venom takes effect the symptoms will become more pronounced with dilation of the pupils, blurred or double vision, slurred speech and difficulty in swallowing. There may also be diarrhoea, blood in the urine and chest or abdominal pain. However you can take comfort from the fact that it takes, on average, 24 hours for death to occur from the time of envenomation.

What Should I do if Someone is Bitten?

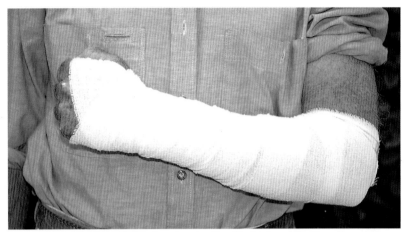

A constrictive bandage is applied to a bite, then the affected limb is immobilised by a sling or splint.

Apply immediate first aid. Do not bother about washing the site of the bite. Do not cut it. Apply a broad constrictive bandage as soon as possible, working from the site of the bite towards the heart. As most bites occur on a limb, as much of the limb as possible should be bound. Wind the bandage firmly but not too tightly.

Immobilise the limb with a splint or a sling. Keep the patient calm and do not administer alcohol. Where practical take transport to the patient and go to for the nearest hospital. Telephone the hospital in advance if possible. Do not remove the bandage or splint. This should be done under medical supervision.

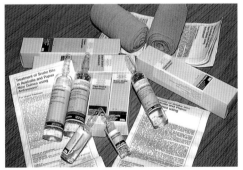

Treatment for venomous snake bites includes pressure bandages and various antivenom kits held by medical institutions.

LEAVE IT TO THE HOSPITAL

It is unnecessary to try and identify the snake or kill it for identification. The hospitals have kits with which they can determine the species of snake responsible. Antivenom comes in two types: monovalent antivenom, which is for a particular species, and polyvalent, which can be used for all the dangerous species of Australian snakes.

Black Snakes

1–2.7m

The Red-bellied Black Snake is usually found near water. Collett's Snake (inset) occurs in drier areas.

There are five species of black snakes, of which the Red-bellied Black Snake is the most well known. However the most widespread is the Mulga (see map) or King Brown Snake, which is actually a member of the black snake family. Except for southern areas and the east coast, this species occurs over most of mainland Australia.

All black snakes are heavy-bodied terrestrial snakes that will flatten out their necks and hiss loudly if disturbed. They are egg-layers, except for the Red-bellied Black Snake, which retains the eggs until full term. These are then laid with just a clear membrane around each young snake. The young break out of this membrane shortly after birth.

Red-bellied Black Snake

The Red-bellied Black Snake has been observed eating eels and trout in the wild and is well known for its fondness of frogs as a meal. As a consequence it has suffered at the hands of the introduced Cane Toad, which is toxic to most animals that mouth or eat it.

Collett's Snake

Collett's Snake is a brightly coloured member of the black snake family that occurs only on the blacksoil plains of central Queensland. It shelters in the deep cracks that occur in the dried soil and is usually active after rain.

A Northern Death Adder showing tail lure.

Death Adders   50cm–1m

Death adders are probably the most easily recognisable of the dangerously venomous snakes. They have a large broad head, a thick short body and a thin tail. There are currently three recognised species that cover most of mainland Australia, apart from southern New South Wales and most of Victoria.

Death adders prefer undisturbed habitat, probably because of their habit of burrowing into leaf litter or into loose sand to lie in wait for prey, such as lizards, birds or small mammals, that may wander past. The tail of all death adders has a soft spine on the tip that is used to lure potential prey close to the snake. The tip of the tail is twitched and wriggled to mimic a grub or caterpillar. When an investigating lizard or bird gets close enough the adder strikes with great speed and accuracy. Because they lie hidden and do not move away when approached, there is always the danger of standing on one.

The Eastern Tiger Snake in defensive mode.

Tiger Snakes   90cm–2.5m

Tiger snakes inhabit the southern areas of Australia, including Tasmania and the Bass Strait islands. There are two species and several subspecies involved. Their names are derived from the banded form of the mainland tiger snake found in southeastern Australia and not because of their disposition. Tiger snakes are generally placid and not easily aroused unless harassed.

This is one group that can flatten out the neck to a considerable degree, giving it an almost cobra-like appearance. Indeed it is sometimes mistaken for a cobra, which although also an elapid, is not found in Australia. The colouring of tiger snakes is extremely variable and depends on the region but it may be black through chocolate to tan or yellow and with or without cross-bands.

The tiger snakes on Chappell Island in Bass Strait can reach a size of almost 2.5 m and are extremely bulky. The snakes on these islands feed predominantly on the chicks of muttonbirds. This means they feed to excess for a few months of the year and starve for the rest of the time.

Brown Snakes

50cm–2.5m

An Eastern Brown Snake is poised to strike in an S-shape coil. Inset: the grey form of the same species.

*B*rown snakes are terrestrial snakes that are active during the day. They are fast moving and bite readily although the fangs are short. All have a more slender body than the black or tiger snakes. There are seven described species of brown snake across Australia and these cover most areas of mainland Australia. The most widespread are the Western Brown Snake (see map) and the Eastern Brown Snake which, together with the Dugite in Western Australia, are the ones most likely to be encountered.

Colour is extremely variable in this group and some individuals are not even brown. The colour can range from grey or tan through various shades of brown to black and there may or may not be bands. This is especially so with the Western Brown Snake, which has nine recognised colour and pattern variations.

The Eastern Brown Snake is adept at concealing itself in grass clumps and will get right down into the roots where it is almost impossible to find. Here it will continue to remain quite still and not retaliate even if it is trodden on.

Breeding and Diet

All brown snakes are egg-layers. They feed on lizards and small mammals. The larger species feed predominantly on mice and so they are attracted to areas where these rodents are numerous. It is for this reason that brown snakes are one of the most common of the dangerous venomous snakes encountered near large population centres. Eastern Brown Snakes are numerous in the western suburbs of Sydney and in Adelaide, and Dugites are the most common venomous snake found in Perth.

Taipans

1–2m

A Common Taipan typically has a long head and a distinct ridge over the eye.

There are two species of Taipan known: the Common Taipan (see map) and the Inland Taipan. Both are active during the day and have been known to grow to a massive size: 2.5 m for the Inland Taipan and 3 m for the Common Taipan, although such lengths are exceptional. The venom of these snakes is extremely potent and they are capable of delivering large quantities, which make them extremely dangerous animals. They are to be avoided at all times. The Common Taipan has a reputation for being aggressive, which is untrue as it is a snake that will avoid contact with people. It will, however, defend itself vigorously if it feels threatened. The Inland Taipan was 'lost' for almost 100 years since it was first described in 1879. It was rediscovered in Queensland in the Windorah area in 1974 and has since been found to occur through western Queensland and northeastern South Australia.

> **WHAT'S IN A NAME?**
> Taipan is the name by which this snake is known to the Aborigines of Cape York. Interestingly, taipan is a Cantonese word for a person of authority.

Taipan Diet

The Common Taipan feeds on mammals, mainly bandicoots, and the Inland Taipan on plague rats. Because of these prey preferences, the snakes need to be able to snap bite accurately and inject a large quantity of venom before letting go. The prey is unable to get far before the venom takes effect. The snake can follow the scent of the victim and eat it without the risk of serious injury.

37

How do Snakes Eat?

*A*ll snakes are carnivorous, that is they eat other animals. They do not eat vegetable matter and generally they catch and eat living prey although instances have been recorded of snakes eating road-killed animals.

Because most cannot dismember their food they must eat it whole, so they select prey that can be swallowed easily or they have adaptations to cope with large prey. In some species the young

The Broad-headed Snake eats lizards whole.

and adults eat the same but different-sized prey. In other species there is a shift as the snake grows. For example, hatchling carpet pythons eat small skinks but the adults eat rats, rabbits, possums, bandicoots and even wallabies.

How do Snakes Digest their Food?

*T*his is where venomous snakes have an advantage over the non-venomous ones because the venom they have helps break down the tissues of the prey and this speeds up digestion. Whether venomous or not, however, snakes still have to keep their body temperature up to aid digestion. If they are too cool, digestion is slowed down and there is a possibility that the prey will rot in the snake's stomach and kill it. That is why when a snake has eaten large prey it will often bask in the sun for extended periods.

A Stimson's Python finishing off a meal of mouse. Food is usually eaten head first.

How do Snakes Swallow Big Animals?

This Bardick has seized a Dtella gecko tail first. Head-first is normally the more successful method but this gecko has already been injected with venom.

Small snakes tend to eat small prey, such as lizards, which do not present them with any problem. Large snakes, however, find it more efficient to take large prey and they must have a way of eating and digesting these.

To achieve this they are able to drop their lower jaw at the back as well as at the front. The lower jaw also stretches sideways as it is joined at the front by a very elastic muscle. This means not only can it stretch its mouth wider horizontally but it can also work one side of its jaw forward independently of the other side. It can literally 'walk' its mouth over its prey using its teeth to anchor and pull. Also a snake's skin is very flexible, allowing it to eat animals that have a larger diameter than itself.

There are other adaptations to help snakes eat large prey. Firstly, their brain is encased in bone; this protects it from the upward kicks of animals while struggling frantically to escape while held in the mouth. Secondly snakes have a tube, called the glottis, in the throat, which is able to project forward beyond the lower jaw so that the snake can breathe while it is eating large prey.

A LARGE MEAL GOES A LONG WAY

The advantage of being able to eat large food items is that you do not have to eat as often. Snakes can go for many months without eating and it is probable that large snakes only eat a few meals each year. It is more efficient to catch and eat one big food item rather than spend a lot of effort catching lots of small animals.

Sea Snakes

50cm–1m

A Stokes Sea Snake foraging for fish in crevices. Inset shows the head of a Shark Bay Sea Snake.

Sea snakes are not eels. Eels are fish with gill slits but no scales or nostrils. The snakes that inhabit the sea are reptiles that have no gill slits but do have scales and nostrils.

There are two distinct groups of sea snakes. The true sea snakes do not come ashore at all, even to the extent that their young are born live at sea. The second group, the sea kraits, do spend some time on land and lay their eggs there. While sea kraits feed on eels, other sea snakes feed on fish and several species have a distinct fondness for fish eggs.

Most sea snakes are dangerously venomous but fortunately they have short fangs and show no inclination to bite if they are left alone. Some are quite curious and will approach divers. This is often assumed to be an aggressive act but there is only a risk of being bitten if the diver kicks out or strikes the snake.

Crevice Foraging and Diving Abilities

Some sea snakes have slender heads and forebodies that thicken out considerably towards the tail. This is an adaptation for foraging into crevices and holes. The snake can poke its thin head and neck into a crevice where fish or eels may be sheltering and easily extract them.

Sea snakes can dive to a depth of 100 m, although a depth of 10–40 m is more normal. They can remain submerged for up to 80 minutes. They can do this because they have enormous elongated lungs that stretch along almost the entire length of their bodies and these can hold a great deal of air.

Yellow-bellied Sea Snake

50cm–1m

A Yellow-bellied Sea Snake showing the distinctive paddle-shaped tail, which is a feature of sea snakes.

All sea snakes inhabit coastal or reef waters except for the Yellow-bellied Sea Snake, which is a truly ocean-going reptile. Great mats of these snakes have been observed far out to sea stretching for kilometres and consisting of many thousands of individuals. The reasons why they congregate in this manner is unknown but it is thought to be associated with ocean slicks and the fish that gather there.

Although the Yellow-bellied Sea Snake occurs in the Pacific and Indian Oceans, it does not inhabit the Atlantic, probably because of the colder water at the southern tip of South America and Africa. Because it stays near the surface of the water it is at the mercy of heavy seas: it can be carried far from its usual haunts and is often washed up on beaches after storms. It has been found as far south as Tasmania and New Zealand.

A NASTY MEAL

While sea snakes often feature in the diets of sharks, particularly tiger sharks, if it is eaten the Yellow-bellied Sea Snake will be regurgitated by predators. There are several instances of marine creatures dying after eating this snake so it appears that the skin or flesh of the Yellow-bellied Sea Snake is toxic.

Going Backwards to Feed

The Yellow-bellied Sea Snake has an interesting strategy for catching fish. Because it is ocean-going it cannot hunt for fish in caves and holes. In the open ocean small fish will often gather around an object that is on or near the surface. In this case they will congregate near the tail of the snake. When it wants a meal the snake swims in reverse, the fish suddenly find themselves at the wrong end, and the snake gets a feed.

Why do Snakes Flick their Tongues Out?

Like snakes, goannas also have forked tongues, which they extend as they taste the air for food scents.

*W*hat snakes lack in hearing they compensate for in having a very advanced sense of smell and taste. Their tongues are constantly flicking in and out and picking up minute chemical particles in the air and on the ground. These are transferred to the Jacobson's organ located in the roof of its mouth. This organ carries out an analysis of the smell and taste of the particles.

The only other reptiles that have forked tongues are goannas and they also flick them in and out constantly to taste the air as they move around.

Can Reptiles Hear?

*S*nakes have no external ears but they do have an inner ear mechanism. So, although they cannot hear, they can apparently pick up vibrations from the ground through their lower jaw. So making a lot of noise as you walk through the bush is unlikely to scare away snakes but they can usually sense your approach if you walk heavily and will slink away into the bush.

A Central Bearded Dragon. The external ear opening is visible above the beard.

Crocodiles can hear and have a well-developed middle and inner ear that helps them to exactly locate possible prey. Hearing is well-developed in many groups of lizards but they probably rely more on sight and movement rather than on sound. Turtles have no external ears but they do have middle ears, which are just below the surface of the skin. They can hear but not as well as crocodiles or lizards.

How Good is Reptilian Sight?

A Golden-tailed Gecko showing the large gecko eye and the vertical pupil of nocturnal foragers.

Vision varies considerably between reptile groups. Snakes that are active during the day and hunt fast-moving prey usually have large eyes and good vision. For other snakes vision is not so important and most do not see that well, probably just moving objects. Blind snakes have very little use for vision and can only distinguish between light and dark.

Crocodiles have their eyes close together, which gives them binocular vision. They use this to precisely locate their prey. Their underwater vision on the other hand is not good. Turtles have good vision. Their eyes can adjust for use on land or in the water. For the majority of lizards vision is an important sense and whether they hunt by day or night their vision is generally good.

A crocodile's binocular vision is perfect for snatching prey out of water.

BIG EYES, LITTLE EYES

Nocturnal mammals and birds generally have large eyes and this is also true of nocturnal lizards, such as geckos, because they rely on sight to locate their food. Nocturnal snakes, however, mostly have small eyes, usually smaller than their daytime relatives. The Brown Tree Snake is an exception as it has very large eyes but most snakes rely on taste and smell to locate prey, and so have no need for good vision and hence large eyes.

CROCODILES

How Much can a Crocodile Eat?

A crocodile's stomach is not huge and a large crocodile can eat 20–40 kg of meat, which is all its stomach will hold. This has led to the story that crocodiles do not eat all of their prey but jam some under logs or in crevices etc. Whether or not they 'store' food is unknown. They may return to previously uneaten food to feed again but then it may be that the meat has attracted fish and turtles, which are fresh food for the crocodile. Larger crocodiles will

scavenge, leaving the water if necessary to take dead animals on land. They will often drag the carcass back to the water before eating it.

A Saltwater Crocodile snatches a fish from an angler's fishing line.

How do Crocodiles Catch Prey?

C rocodiles are most active at night, which is when most of their feeding occurs. However crocodiles are opportunistic feeders and will feed during the day if a meal presents itself. Most prey is caught in the shallows at the water's edge, particularly with young crocodiles, which will snap at anything that disturbs the water near them. Adults will wait in the shallow water for suitable prey to come down to the edge but they will also spot potential prey at a distance and approach underwater until they are within striking range.

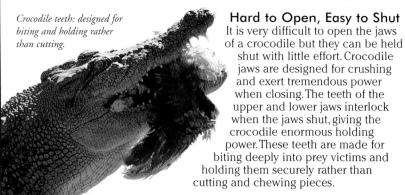

Crocodile teeth: designed for biting and holding rather than cutting.

Hard to Open, Easy to Shut
It is very difficult to open the jaws of a crocodile but they can be held shut with little effort. Crocodile jaws are designed for crushing and exert tremendous power when closing. The teeth of the upper and lower jaws interlock when the jaws shut, giving the crocodile enormous holding power. These teeth are made for biting deeply into prey victims and holding them securely rather than cutting and chewing pieces.

How do Crocodiles Get Rid of Salt?

In Saltwater Crocodiles salt is removed from the body via special salt glands on the tongue.

Crocodiles swallow salt water with their food. To get rid of the excess salt through the kidneys would require large amounts of fresh water, which is often unavailable, so they have adopted a different strategy. They have salt glands on the tongue that excrete a highly salty solution.

> **SIZE AND LIFESPAN**
>
> Saltwater Crocodiles are the largest of all living crocodiles and alligators. While a 4-m crocodile is regarded as a large one, they are reputed to grow to 6 m long. They may live to 100 years old.

How Common are Crocodile Attacks?

When someone gets killed by a crocodile it receives a great deal of media attention but how many people do get taken by crocodiles in Australia? Prior to 1972 there are no accurate records but between 1972 and 1988 there were 13 fatalities or near fatalities. Of these, two occurred between 1972 and 1979 and 11 occurred between 1980 and 1988. Of these 13 attacks, 10 were on people swimming, of which half were at night. Put into perspective, crocodile attacks are very few and many are the result of foolishness and bravado on the part of the people concerned.

> **SWIMMING CROCS**
>
> Crocodiles swim by using their strong tails in a sideways movement. Although the hindlimbs are webbed between the claws, they are of little use in propelling the crocodile through the water and are held against the body.

Freshwater Crocodile   1.5m

An adult Freshwater Crocodile basking in the shallow water. They will bite if they are harassed.

The Freshwater Crocodile is smaller than the Saltwater Crocodile and has a narrow snout. It feeds on such prey as frogs, shrimps, fish and insects but will take anything of a suitable size. It is not regarded as dangerous to swimmers, although children would need to be closely watched. Freshwater Crocodiles can bite and will do so if harassed.

Found only in the northern part of Australia, the Freshwater Crocodile inhabits permanent freshwater swamps, billabongs and rivers. It may also move into the tidal areas of some rivers, apparently where the Saltwater Crocodiles are absent or low in numbers.

Nesting and Growth

During the dry season a female crocodile digs out a nest on a sandbank, lays her eggs and then covers it over with sand. Several females may use the same area to nest, so sometimes a nest of eggs will be excavated by another female as she digs her own nest. When they are born, the young call from the nest and are dug out by an adult female, who will then carry them to the water in her mouth. Females will remain with groups of hatchlings for several weeks, apparently to protect them from predators. During this period they are quite aggressive.

In the upper reaches of the Liverpool River in Arnhem Land in the Northern Territory, the Freshwater Crocodiles exhibit extremely stunted growth. This seems to be related to their habitat, which is somewhat rocky and lacking in food. Although they are mature, the crocodiles here are considerably smaller, in both size and weight, than those found on the coastal plains where food is more plentiful.

Saltwater Crocodile

2–4m

Saltwater Crocodiles spend a lot of time out of the water, raising their body temperature to a level where they can hunt effectively. These crocodiles will kill and eat people and should be avoided.

The Saltwater Crocodile is a far more formidable animal than its freshwater relative, and it does eat people. While normally found in estuaries and tidal rivers, these crocodiles also inhabit fresh water and will go out to sea. The smaller Saltwater Crocodiles feed on insects, frogs, small fish and reptiles. The larger ones will eat fish, birds, reptiles and whatever other suitably sized animals they can get, including wallabies.

HOT EGGS, COLD EGGS

The sex of a crocodile is determined by the temperature at which its egg was incubated. Eggs in a nest will not all be incubating at the same heat: those at the bottom may be cooler because it is damper, or they may be hotter because they are in the middle of the rotting vegetation. Embryos incubated at high or low temperatures will become females, while those incubated at mid-range temperatures will become males.

Mortality in the nest

In the wet season females construct a nest of vegetation and soil and lay their eggs within. The eggs are left to incubate in the heat generated by the rotting vegetation. Mortality of eggs in nests is high, often because flooding covers the eggs with water and the embryos drown. The females remain near their nests and will defend them from intruders. It has been estimated that about 20 per cent of the eggs laid in a season actually hatch, and less than 1 per cent will reach maturity. As with Freshwater Crocodiles, the female will remove hatchlings from the nest and take them to the water.

TURTLES

Marine Turtles

The Loggerhead Turtle: the limbs of marine turtles are more like flippers than legs.

Of the six species of marine turtles that occur in Australian waters, only the Flatback Turtle is confined to this region. The other five species are the Loggerhead, Green, Leathery, Hawkesbill and Pacific Ridley Turtles.

All marine turtles come ashore to lay their eggs in a hole dug by the female above the high-water mark on a beach. The hole is then filled in with sand and the eggs left to incubate. Depending on the species, females will lay several clutches of eggs in a season over a period of weeks. The young of a clutch emerge from their eggs simultaneously and move in a group towards the surface.

Back to the Water

If the sand is hot they will wait just below the surface until it cools down, indicating the sun has set. During the night or early morning they emerge from the sand and make for the water. Because it is generally lighter over the water at night they use this to find their way. If there are brighter lights on the land they can become disorientated and get lost. Despite the darkness, baby turtles are heavily predated upon by seabirds, crabs and fish.

Once in the water, they seem to disappear. Little is known about where they go for their first decade of life but at about 10 years of age they reappear in the feeding grounds with the larger turtles. It is thought that perhaps they go way out to sea to avoid the predators that are more numerous in the shallow waters.

A female Green Turtle coming ashore to lay her eggs.

Green Turtle 1.5m

The Green Turtle is a vegetarian and feeds on seagrasses and seaweeds. This is the turtle that people catch for food and is the main ingredient of turtle soup. Its shell is also used to make jewellery, although 'tortoiseshell' is more popular and this is derived from the shell of the Hawkesbill Turtle.

A female Green Turtle will lay about 110 soft-shelled eggs at a time. She may return to the beach three or four times to lay during the season but Green Turtles do not breed every year and three or more years may pass between nestings. They normally emerge from the sea to lay their eggs only after dark. They will also try to come ashore with the high tide or shortly after, as this means they do not have to travel so far up the beach before digging the nest.

The Leathery Turtle has distinctive ridges along the length of its shell. It is massive and can weigh 500 kg.

Leathery Turtle 2m

The Leathery Turtle is the largest of the turtles: it can reach a length of 2 m and a weight of over 500 kg. It is unlike the other marine turtles in that it does not have a hard bony shell but one which looks and feels more like hard rubber and has seven ridges running along it.

Like all adult marine turtles, the Leathery Turtle has specific feeding areas that may be thousands of kilometres from its breeding and nesting areas and it will return to the same nesting beaches in successive breeding seasons. The Leathery Turtle is the most migratory of the turtles and holds the record for the longest migration of any turtle: a distance of 5900 km.

Leathery Turtles feed mainly on jellyfish. They can dive to depths of 1000 m and stay underwater for 60 minutes by storing large quantities of oxygen in their blood and muscles.

TURTLE TEETH AND TUCKER

Turtles do not have teeth; only hard bony ridges. If a turtle's diet consists of shellfish and crustaceans, the ridges are used to crush the food. If they are consumers of seagrasses, sponges and similar soft food, then they can shear like scissors. The Leathery Turtle has two deep notches in the jaw that help it to hold jellyfish.

Do Marine Turtles have Special Adaptations?

Hatchling Green Turtles have large and powerful forelimbs.

Marine turtles are adapted to a life at sea in many ways. The forelimbs are powerful flippers that enable the turtle to fly through the water. They have glands to get rid of excess salt that accumulates in the body. Their shells look very heavy and cumbersome but are in fact light and streamlined, and the shell is honeycombed to reduce its weight. Only the females return to land, and then they do so only to lay their eggs.

How Often do Marine Turtles Breed?

It is thought that marine turtles take many years before they start to breed; estimates vary from 10 to 50 years. Even then they may only breed every two to eight years and, although they can lay several hundred eggs in a season, fewer than one in one thousand hatchlings survives to maturity. As with crocodiles, the sex of hatchlings is determined by temperature: those eggs incubated at the higher range develop as females, while those at the lower range become males. Mid-range temperatures produce both males and females. If turtles reach adult size, they probably live for a very long time and will hopefully produce enough offspring to replace themselves.

OUR NATIVE TURTLE

The Flatback Turtle of northern Australia feeds on jellyfish and soft coral and nests in isolated areas in the Gulf of Carpentaria and the Torres Strait. Unlike other species, young Flatback Turtles do not 'disappear' into the ocean, rather they stay around coastal waters.

Only one in a thousand marine turtle hatchlings will survive to maturity.

Do Turtles Hibernate?

*F*reshwater turtles will hibernate during the cool winter months in south-eastern Australia. Depending on the species and locality this may involve settling into mud and debris at the bottom of a pool or coming out of water onto the land and hibernating beneath leaves or litter in some moist spot. Turtles will also become inactive if their waterhole dries up.

In such cases they will dig into the mud at the bottom of the drying pool and stay there in a form of hibernation until the pool fills up with water again. If this fails to happen within a reasonable period the turtles will die.

Captive 'pet shop' turtles are known to hibernate.

THE PET SHOP TURTLE

New species of freshwater turtles are still being discovered. John Cann, the authority on Australian freshwater turtles, spent 20 years tracking down the locality of the 'pet shop' turtle. This turtle was known only from hatchlings which were sold in pet shops in the 1970s. After many false leads John eventually found these turtles in the Mary River in Queensland, which is their only known location.

Which is Australia's Rarest Turtle?

*T*he Western Swamp Turtle in Western Australia is one of the most endangered Australian reptiles. There are probably less than 150 animals alive and they live only in a few small temporary swamps near Perth. An intensive captive-breeding program has increased the existing population but it still remains extremely vulnerable because of the low numbers and its precarious lifestyle.

The Western Swamp Turtle, at an average length of about 12 cm, is the smallest Australian turtle.

Freshwater Turtles

The Manning River Turtle is a short-necked turtle found in the rivers of northern New South Wales.

There are 17 species of freshwater turtles in Australia and all except one belong to a group known as side-necked turtles because the neck is folded under the carapace with one or more horizontal folds. Within this group some have very long necks and are known as long-necked or snake-necked turtles. The others are collectively called short-necked turtles.

Habitat and Feeding

Most bodies of freshwater are likely to have some freshwater turtles for they are found over much of mainland Australia. Some prefer the slow-flowing deeper inland rivers, while others are found in the rapid-flowing clear rivers on the coast. Indeed on the east coast each river drainage seems to carry its own distinct freshwater turtle; some have not yet been scientifically described.

Some freshwater turtles feed mainly on plant material while others are carnivorous, taking crustaceans, shellfish, insects, snails and any other suitably sized animals they can seize. Their extendable necks allow them to breathe while keeping their bodies submerged. These turtles feed in the water, some using the long neck to strike at prey. The Broad-shelled Turtle, for example, relies on ambush to procure its food; buried in debris on the river bottom, it lunges its head and neck forward to take its prey.

Predation

The nests of freshwater turtles are constructed near water and the eggs deposited and left there. These nests are subject to very heavy predation and it is estimated that more than 90 per cent of eggs are taken, by foxes, pigs, feral cats and dogs, goannas and water rats. Baby turtles fall prey to birds, fish, crocodiles and eels and, even when they grow larger, feral dogs, cats and foxes, as well as crocodiles, remain a threat.

An Eastern Long-necked Turtle gliding underwater.

Eastern Long-necked Turtle

One of the better known turtles is the Eastern Long-necked or Snake-necked Turtle, which is widely distributed and found in swamps and river systems. Hatchlings of this species are black, with orange on their undersides. It is not known how long this turtle lives in the wild but there is a record of one kept in captivity for 36 years.

The Eastern Long-necked Turtle, which reaches a length of 25 cm, is the most southerly occurring freshwater turtle in Australia. It can carry out extensive overland migrations in summer in search of new water bodies and is sometimes seen wandering across paddocks or even down roads as it treks towards a new location. It is notorious for its musk gland secretion that is quite offensive to people. Thought to be an anti-predator device, it invariably occurs when wild turtles are handled. Animals that have been kept in captivity for some time are less likely to do this.

A Pig-nosed Turtle shows its pig-like snout.

Pig-nosed Turtle   60cm

The Pig-nosed Turtle differs from other Australian turtles in having a shell covered with a soft, pitted skin and paddle-like limbs similar to marine turtles, rather than clawed, webbed feet. As the name suggests it has a prominent pig-like nose. It occurs in New Guinea and in a few river systems in northern Australia, and feeds mainly on seeds, fruits and leaves that fall into the water; it will also take fish and shellfish. The Pig-nosed Turtle lays up to 20 eggs in a nest on a sandbank in the river and the young stay within the eggs until the nest is flooded by rising water. They then emerge and swim away.

Unlike all other Australian freshwater turtles, which must twist their necks sideways to retract their heads, the Pig-nosed Turtle can pull its head straight back into its shell.

> **'BOOF-HEADED' TURTLES**
> Some turtles develop a condition in which the head becomes greatly enlarged. Such 'boof-headed' turtles are the result of continual shellfish crushing and such a deformity is most pronounced in older turtles.

LIZARDS

How do Geckos Differ from Skinks?

*T*here are many differences between these two major groups of lizards. For example, geckos are mainly active at night while the majority of skinks are active during the day. You would be very unlikely to find a gecko foraging out in the open during the day, although you might find one sheltering under cover.

The Southern Sandslider, a burrowing skink of soft sands, has only a pair of hindlimbs and these are very small.

Geckos are soft-bodied and quite delicate in appearance, although some have spines and tubercles on their scales. The scales are not shiny at all nor do they overlap. The skin of many geckos is quite translucent, particularly on the belly, and the unlaid eggs of female geckos are clearly visible through their body wall. Skinks, on the other hand, have hard overlapping scales, which in many species are shiny.

Body and Clutch Sizes

Geckos as a group tend to be small, the largest species being only about 30 cm long. They also have large eyes in proportion to the rest of their body, which is to be expected because they are nocturnal animals that rely on sight when foraging. Skinks range from 10 to 60 cm in length and their eyes are not noticeably prominent. All geckos have four well-developed limbs with five digits. Skinks may have four to no limbs and often these are small, with one to five small digits. In many geckos the digits are expanded and pad-like so they can climb smooth surfaces.

In Australia all geckos are egg-layers and for most the clutch size is two, although a few lay only one. Skinks may be egg-layers or live-bearers but the clutch sizes of egg-layers are normally more than two.

The big-eyed Giant Cave Gecko forages at night.

Why do Geckos Lick their Eyes?

Geckos do not have eyelids: instead the eye is covered with a transparent scale which comes off when the skin is shed. They are often seen wiping their eyes with their tongue. This is how they clean their eye scales. The majority of skinks, on the other hand, have movable eyelids and they do not usually wipe their eyes with their tongues.

This Northern Velvet Gecko wipes its eye scales with its tongue to keep them free from dust and dirt particles.

Which Lizards Walk on Ceilings?

Some geckos are able to walk across apparently smooth surfaces and even upside down on ceilings. This ability to traverse ceilings and glass windows is aided by highly specialised toes. These toes have a series of enlarged plate-like suction pads underneath which are called lamellae. Each of the lamellae is covered with microscopic hairs that come into contact with the surface on which the gecko is walking. These hairs or setae actually bond with the surface and the sheer numbers of these setae are sufficient to provide the adhesive force required for the gecko to maintain an upside-down or vertical position on a smooth surface. No skink can perform such feats, nor can all geckos. Some species have strong claws but no enlarged pads at all, although they can still climb vertical surfaces that are rough or irregular.

The underside of the foot of a Marbled Velvet Gecko showing the enlarged lamellae.

> ### REPTILIAN NOISES
> Legless lizards and geckos are the only lizards with an ability to vocalise. The quite audible and rather disconcerting noises emitted by geckos are usually described as squeaks, coughs or barks. No skinks are known to vocalise, although some may produce a noise when roughly handled as air is expelled from their lungs.

Geckos

The Golden-tailed Gecko is a tree-dweller that lives in callitris trees, blending in with the foliage.

We have 102 species of gecko in Australia. These are all nocturnal and they may be ground-dwellers, tree-dwellers, cave- or rock-dwellers. The biggest gecko in Australia is the Ring-tailed Gecko from north-eastern Queensland which grows to more than 30 cm; the smallest is the Clawless Gecko which only grows to about 7.5 cm.

Different Habitats

There are many ground-dwelling geckos and some are quite specialised in their requirements. The Jewelled Gecko, for example, is found only in porcupine grass clumps. It lives within the protection of its spiny leaves and feeds upon invertebrates in and around the clump. The Pilbara Gecko is often found inside large termite mounds in the Pilbara region of Western Australia.

Some geckos have decided that the best place to live is in caves. The Giant Cave Gecko from Arnhem Land, which grows to 20 cm, and the Cave Prickly Gecko, a small 10-cm long species which occurs in areas of Western Australia, are two that utilise caves. They are able to take advantage of the less extreme temperatures in the deep recesses, while preying on the invertebrate inhabitants of the caves.

One of the unusual tree-dwelling geckos is the Leaf-tail Gecko from Queensland, which has a tail shaped exactly like a leaf and a body which is extremely flattened. The colours of this gecko are such that they resemble the lichens that grow on tree trunks in rainforest. Another is the Golden-tailed Gecko, which despite its colours, is well camouflaged in the foliage.

A Marbled Velvet Gecko foraging on a tree.

Velvet Geckos

Some of the most brightly coloured geckos are those known as the velvet geckos because of their soft velvety skin. Several of them, such as the Marbled Velvet Gecko and the Southern Velvet Gecko, grow up to 18 cm long and many of this group live in trees. They all have somewhat flattened bodies so that they can fit comfortably under the bark of dead trees or into crevices in wood or rock. If threatened they raise their tails and slowly move them from side to side, while keeping the rest of the body still.

In some areas, velvet geckos occur in very high densities with one residing in virtually every suitable tree. In most cases, adult velvet geckos do not gather in groups. Although they may occur in pairs as adults and they may tolerate the immature geckos, they will drive away other adults. The Southern Velvet Geckos are exceptional in this respect and it is not uncommon to find six or seven of these rock-dwellers gathered together under a single boulder.

A Smooth Knob-tailed Gecko.

Knob-tailed Geckos

There are seven different species of knob-tailed geckos; together their distribution covers most of central and northern Australia. These large geckos all grow to at least 11 cm and they are quite odd-looking lizards. Their heads are large in proportion to their bodies and tails, and the tails are very short and end in a soft knob. The small tails on these large geckos make them look a bit unbalanced, almost as though parts of the tail are missing. Why the knob is there and what it is used for is unknown.

Knob-tailed geckos are ground-dwellers that inhabit sandy regions of arid Australia and often live in burrows made by themselves or other animals. They eat insects but also prey on other lizards, particularly geckos and skinks.

SEALED IN

The Three-lined Knob-tailed Gecko uses burrows for shelter. It may adopt those of other animals or it may construct a burrow of its own. To protect itself from intruders, it will seal itself into its shelter chamber, closing the entrance off with some loose soil or sand.

What's in a Tail?

Knob-tailed geckos have distinctively shaped tails.

Gecko tails come in many shapes and sizes and they are put to a number of uses by their owners. They may use them to store reserves of fat in times of plenty and it has been suggested that those with fat tails are better able to store reserves than those with thin tails. All geckos have the ability, too, to discard or shed their tails when threatened and most will do this readily. Tail-shedding is a feature that normally occurs when the gecko is active but it has been found that in several of the geckos tail loss will happen even in cold weather when the gecko is inactive. At such times it is more usual for the whole tail to be shed and not just the minimum amount needed to make an escape. Although this response must be an attempt to distract a predator, it is strange behaviour for a cold gecko that is unable to move quickly, if at all. Perhaps by discarding the tail the gecko is able to move more quickly because it is a lot lighter without the weight of its tail.

This Bynoes Prickly Gecko has lost its tail and regrown a completely new one of a different colour.

Why do Geckos Twitch their Tails?

The Southern Leaf-tail Gecko will elevate and twitch its tail.

Slow waving or twitching of the tail is used by some geckos when stalking prey. This diverts the attention of its prey while the gecko gets close enough to pounce. In other species the tail is elevated and waved slowly from side to side when the gecko is threatened. This will focus a predator's attention on the moving tail and hopefully it will lunge at the tail instead of the body. The gecko can then drop its tail, which will wriggle quite vigorously when detached, and make its escape.

Tails as Weapons and Supports

One group of geckos, known collectively as the spiny-tailed geckos, have the ability to squirt a sticky liquid from spines situated on their tails. This substance is ejected for several centimetres and may confuse or irritate a predator long enough for a gecko to make its escape. In some cases the fluid oozes rather than squirts and it is probable that in these cases the gecko wipes the substance onto the predator with its tail.

Tail-gripping Geckos

One group of arboreal geckos from northern Australia, known as the pad-tailed geckos have grasping tails that are adapted for clinging onto branches and so provide the geckos with extra support as they forage in the trees or shrubs. The tips of the tails are also modified in that they are equipped with suction pads or lamellae similar to those found on the undersurfaces of these geckos' feet. These assist in providing the gecko with increased mobility and better holding ability when it is climbing over difficult surfaces.

> **RAINING TAILS**
> The story goes that many years ago some collectors were staying in a hut where there were a lot of geckos in the roof. Unable to catch them, they decided to fire a gun to frighten the geckos so they would drop to the floor. Not so — when the gun was fired the geckos discarded their tails which rained down onto the floor.

The Northern Spiny-tailed Gecko squirts sticky stuff from the spines on its tail.

How do Reptiles Protect Themselves?

A Jewelled Gecko on a spinifex clump. These geckos can release a sticky fluid from the tail to deter predators.

Apart from the more obvious defence of biting, which almost all reptiles will do — and snakes have enhanced with the added deterrent of venom — reptiles have evolved a range of mechanisms to avoid predation.

Some turtles and snakes will release a very strong-smelling odour when handled that is certainly objectionable to our noses and presumably unpleasant to other predators, too. Some geckos, such as the Spiny-tailed Gecko, can squirt or exude a sticky liquid from spines on their tails. This comes out as fine threads that can adhere to a predator and cause some discomfort.

The colour of many reptiles is such that they blend in perfectly with their background. Some reptiles can change colour to enhance this effect. Combined with staying still this will often reduce predation or detection. The death adders are a good example of this, as is the Leaf-tailed Gecko.

Mimicry is another useful defence method and is used by the Common Scalyfoot Lizard, which will inflate its neck and raise its head and neck up like a snake. Some lizards, particularly newborn ones, have bands and colours that make them look like venomous snakes.

The Desert Death Adder protects itself by concealment.

SNAKES ALIVE!

The crowned snakes have an interesting defence pose. When threatened a crowned snake will raise its head and neck off the ground and turn the top of its head down towards the threat, thereby displaying the crown on the top of its head. Perhaps this resembles the open mouth of a larger snake and is designed to intimidate the predator.

Do all Reptiles Drop their Tails?

A Common Garden Skink with a regenerated tail plus the original tail which did not sever completely.

*T*ail shedding is common in many reptiles, particularly geckos, skinks and legless lizards. It is not used by dragons or goannas and very rarely found in snakes. This strategy involves shedding all or part of the tail if handled roughly, particularly if the tail itself is grasped. The discarded tail will wriggle and thrash around for some time, which distracts the predator and allows the lizard to escape.

The tail breaks at certain points along its length and will regrow from that point. Sometimes the tail only partially breaks and this will mean that when a new tail grows from that point there are two tails. There have even been lizards found with three tails. Regrown tails can be distinguished from originals as they usually have a different colour or are a different texture. It is not uncommon to find lizards in the wild with regenerated tails, so this defence mechanism is obviously one that is commonly used.

Why do some Reptiles have Prickly Skins?

*S*cales that are very rough or prickly make a good defence mechanism. When a predator picks up a prickly reptile it causes irritation to its mouth. Some, such as the Gidgee Skink and Cunningham's Skink, which have this feature, also inflate their bodies to wedge themselves tightly into rock crevices or cracks in timber. Inflating the body to look bigger and bluff an enemy into leaving them alone is a strategy also employed by bearded dragons, bluetongues and black snakes.

The tail of a Gidgee Skink has sharp spines to discourage predators.

Legless Lizards

Mallee Worm-lizard, a little known legless lizard, which uses ant nests for shelter and food.

Legless lizards, or pygopods as they are sometimes called, are unique to Australia and New Guinea. They are quite diverse in appearance, some being worm-like and others very snake-like. They range in size from 15 cm to 85 cm and are closely related to the geckos, with whom they share the ability to vocalise and to wipe their eyes with their tongues.

The Representatives

The 10 worm-like members of the group are small and, as they live underground most of the time, they are very rarely seen. Their bodies are the same width all the way to their rounded tail and they have well-developed eyes, which is surprising for lizards that live under the ground. Several of these lizards have bright pink or red tails that may serve to divert a predator's attack to the tail rather than the head.

Other legless lizards belong to the *Delma* group. Most numerous of the legless lizards, there are 17 species known and one or another are found over much of Australia. They have two small flaps near the vent that represent the remnants of hindlimbs. These legless lizards engage in flick leaping to escape a predator. This involves the lizard in flicking itself into the air and at the same time propelling itself forward. It is done very rapidly and makes the lizard a very difficult target for any predator to catch.

BRONZEBACK REDISCOVERED

The Bronzeback Legless Lizard was first found in the 1890s and was not seen again until 1978 when two amateur herpetologists found several under the leaf litter beneath wattle shrubs. Since then the Bronzeback has been found at several more localities but remains poorly known.

Burton's Legless Lizard

One of the colour patterns of Burton's Legless Lizard.

The most commonly encountered legless lizard is Burton's Legless Lizard, which is very snake like in appearance and in its habits. It has a long wedge-shaped snout and it is unique among the legless lizards in that it eats other lizards. As far as is known, all other legless lizards eat invertebrates. This lizard will lie in wait under cover or in a grass clump and pounce on a skink or dragon that passes close by. It is active during the day and at night when it has been seen loosely coiled in the top of porcupine grass waiting to ambush geckos. As with all legless lizards, it is an egg-layer with two eggs to a clutch.

Burton's Legless Lizard is unusual for a legless lizard in that it comes in a whole range of colours and patterns, which are so different that you would think they are completely separate species. It is also one of only two legless lizards that occur outside Australia, with New Guinea being its other home.

Scaly-foot Lizards

A Southern Scaly-foot carrying out a threat display.

The other group that is most commonly seen are the scaly-foots, of which there are three species that between them cover most of mainland Australia. They have quite noticeable leg flaps and are all robust in build. The Southern Scaly-foot is the largest of the legless lizards and can grow to 85 cm. The western and eastern species are not as large and are both recognisable by the black 'hood' on their head and neck. They are predominantly spider eaters and while the Southern Scaly-foot is active during the day and at dusk, the western and eastern forms are nocturnal.

When threatened scaly-foots will raise their heads and forebodies up off the ground and flatten their necks in a manner that mimics an elapid snake. They will carry this further by striking. This display is a bluff but it may stop a potential predator from coming any closer.

Legless Lizard or Snake?

*U*nfortunately many of the legless lizards look like snakes and suffer the consequences. It can be difficult for people unfamiliar with reptiles to tell the difference but once seen they are quite recognisable as not being snakes.

It is true that some of the legless lizards are very worm-like but so are several of the snakes. The snake-like legless lizards are not distinguishable by colour alone but their tongues, ears and tails bear obvious external differences and some behavioural traits are also distinct.

Features and Traits

The tongue of a legless lizard is broad and fleshy with a small notch, whereas that of a snake is long, slender and forked. Legless lizards will use their tongues to wipe their eyes but snakes cannot do this although a snake's tongue is constantly flicked in and out.

Most, but not all, of the legless lizards have external ear openings; these are absent in snakes. The ear openings are most obvious in the larger legless lizards and are situated behind and slightly below each eye.

The tail in legless lizards is considerably longer than in snakes and, in some cases it is much longer than the body itself. (A tail begins at the anus or vent.) It is also easily cast off if the lizard is handled roughly or grasped by the tail. Snakes, with the exception of the Freshwater Snake, do not cast off their tails and they are always much shorter than their bodies. The tails of a legless lizard will regrow. If a snake loses its tail it will not regrow. Any replacement tail is usually noticeable because of the difference in colour or pattern.

A scaly-foot lizard licks its eye. Behind the mouth, the ear opening is quite visible.

On a Microscopic Scale

Few people would ever be close enough to notice but there are differences in the scales of snakes and legless lizards. Those on the belly of most snakes are broad and much larger than those on the rest of the body. In many of the legless lizards these belly scales are only slightly wider than the adjacent scales.

Closeup of the belly scales of a snake.

Did Legless Lizards Once Have Legs?

A flap of skin and bone on the side of this Southern Scaly-foot's body is all that remains of its hindlimb.

*I*t seems likely that legless lizards once had legs. The remnants of hindlimbs are undoubtedly present in the legless lizards, although in some species they are no more than a very small flap only slightly larger than the adjacent scales. These flaps are normally inconspicuous and are tucked against the side of the body but sometimes they are used by the lizard to aid movement through grass clumps and are positioned at right angles to the body.

The limb flap of the Scaly-foot held away from the body. The flap actually contains leg bones.

Legless lizards shared a common ancestor with geckos but somewhere along the line one group decided life without legs was a better option and so legless lizards evolved. There are also skinks that have reduced the number or size of their legs or have no legs at all. They have evolved this way, however, quite independently and do not belong to the same lineage. It is not uncommon in the animal kingdom for members of different lineages to develop similar adaptations in order to exploit similar environments. Snakes, too, have taken the limbless option.

Who are the Dragons?

*A*ll 65 species of dragons known in Australia are active during the day, lay eggs and have a rough skin that often has spines or tubercles. They all have well-developed limbs and can move quickly. Males of many species are more brightly coloured than females, especially in the breeding season. Most are desert-dwellers but there are exceptions, such as the two species of rainforest dragon and the Eastern Water Dragon. These occupy more humid and higher rainfall regions.

Long-tailed Earless Dragons from the arid regions make use of rocks to survey their territory.

Why are Reptiles the Colour They Are?

*R*eptiles can recognise colour but to what extent varies considerably between groups. Colour recognition is obviously well developed in lizards because the males of many species develop bright colours during the mating season to attract females and to deter rivals. The females, on the other hand, are usually quite drab in colour. This colour difference between the sexes is most obvious in the dragons and in some of the smaller skinks.

In snakes colour differences between the sexes is not usual. Colour vision in snakes is limited and snakes do not defend territories in the same way as lizards. The male lizard uses colour to attract the female but in snakes the males usually move around widely in the mating season to find and mate with females. Vivid colours would serve no purpose in this situation.

Male Painted Dragon displaying bright colours to attract a female.

When is Colour Cool?

*E*ven though colouring is not of any great consequence in the mating game, many snakes are brightly coloured and patterned. The Bandy Bandy is boldly ringed in black and white. If one is uncovered it is immediately obvious but in its usual underground habitat colour is probably of no consequence. When the snake makes occasional forays to the surface at night, the black and white bands disrupt its outline, making it more difficult to see in subdued

Colourful Southern Desert Banded Snake.

light. In fact, many burrowing snakes, which tend to be small and nocturnal, bear brightly coloured bands. Besides breaking up their outline, the colours may bluff a predator into believing that it is dealing with a dangerous snake.

Do Reptiles Change Colour ?

*C*olours can differ between juveniles and adults, both in lizards and snakes. Juveniles are often a lot brighter than their adult counterparts. In Eastern Brown Snakes, for example, the juveniles have a black head and often they have bands some or all the way down their bodies; these disappear as the snake grows. In the Blue-bellied Black Snakes the juveniles are a silver grey colour, while adults are usually plain black. Most dramatically, juvenile Green Pythons, which are yellow or red, change to green within their first few years.

Some reptiles change colour in response to temperature variations. The bearded

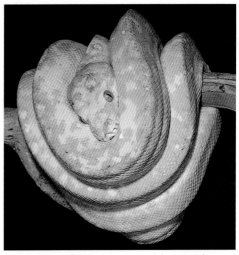

A young Green Python in the process of changing colour from yellow to the bright green of adults.

dragons are dark in colour but lighten quickly when they warm up. Some snakes change colour depending on the season: the Inland Taipan, for example, has a black head in the cooler months but loses this coloration in summer. This helps it heat up more quickly in winter, not so much during summer.

Small Dragons

Red-barred Crevice Dragon from the Flinders Ranges. Males perch predominantly on rocks.

One of the smaller dragons that is commonly seen over much of central Australia is the Central Netted Dragon. It is conspicuous because of its habit of perching on top of stumps, rocks or other elevated sites. Road spoil heaped along the sides of dirt roads is often used for this purpose.

An interesting group of dragons are the crevice dragons, most of which occur in South Australia. There are six species known and in all of these the females are quite drab in colour. The males, on the other hand, are much more colourful, particularly during the breeding season when they display prominently.

The slender two-line dragons from northern Australia and the southern desert areas have tails that are more than twice their body length. Perched in low vegetation, they are very hard to detect.

The Mallee Dragon

The Mallee Dragon is a little dragon that has an interesting life history. It occurs in association with porcupine grass and mallee. Most animals in a population will live for only 12 months with a few surviving into the next year. The number that do survive appears to be directly related to the success rate in hatchlings. If conditions are harsh and many eggs fail to hatch, a greater number of adults will survive to the next breeding season.

> **A LIVING STONE**
> The Blotch-tailed Earless Dragon, a dumpy little lizard with a short tail, is found in arid and semi-arid stony areas. It looks exactly like a wind-polished pebble and merges into the ground among the pebbles so well that it is almost undetectable when still.

An Eastern Water Dragon: largest of our dragons.

Eastern Water Dragon   1m

The Eastern Water Dragon is the largest of the Australian dragons and males can reach a metre in length. They are unusual in that they inhabit watercourses, whereas most of our dragons are found in arid regions. They are territorial and a male will have a territory along a creek or river in which only the females are free to move. In some areas they will spend the nights during summer submerged in the water hanging onto the bank with only their heads exposed. In such a situation a predator would find it difficult to attack, and escape into deep water is an easy option for the dragon. A female will dig several 'trial' burrows before deciding where to lay her 6–12 eggs. The burrow she digs may be up to 11 cm deep and after she has laid her eggs she replaces the soil and covers the site with leaves.

A Frilled Lizard displaying to warn off a threat.

Frilled Lizard   95cm

The Frilled Lizard is another large dragon. It is well known to most people as it features on the two-cent coin. During normal activities this lizard's frill is folded back and it can be quite inconspicuous on the trunk of a tree as it merges in well against the bark. The frill is only used if the dragon is threatened.

At such times, the dragon opens its mouth to show a wide gape, hoping to scare off the perceived threat. The action of opening the mouth causes the frill to extend; this apparent increase in size is designed to intimidate the threat still further. Because the frill contains long rod-like bones that connect with the jaw and tongue, the wider the mouth is opened the more extended the frill from the neck muscles becomes. If all else fails, the Frilled Lizard can take to its hindlegs and run in a short high-speed dash in order to escape.

Thorny Devil slowly moving to an ant trail.

Thorny Devil 20cm

Australian dragons come in all shapes and sizes and there are some quite bizarre ones. Most people have seen pictures of the Thorny Devil, which is a small dragon from central and western Australia. Despite its very spiky appearance it is quite harmless, the spines and thorns protecting it from predators. It has a small head and a prominent hump on the back of its neck, the purpose of which is unclear but since it lowers its head when frightened, presenting the spiky hump to the would-be predator, it possibly acts as a defence mechanism.

Thorny Devils have an almost mechanical jerky gait and are slow moving. They live entirely on small black ants and will sit by an ant trail simply eating them as they run past. They are able to drink by taking up water along capillary grooves on the skin that lead the water to the mouth. In this way they maximise water uptake from light showers or even dew.

Boyd's Forest Dragon showing its defensive display.

Rainforest Dragons

The rainforest dragons are unusual in that they occur in rainforests and not in arid areas like others. Measuring between 30 and 40 cm, there are only two species in Australia, and both occur along the coastal regions of New South Wales and Queensland. They spend most of their time up trees, usually only about two metres off the ground. Rainforest dragons have great camouflage, merging in well with the tree trunk so that they are extremely difficult to detect. They also have a habit of moving skillfully, almost invisibly, to the other side of a tree trunk from any curious observer.

TERRITORIAL DISPLAYS

Most male dragons perform threat displays towards other male dragons encroaching on their territory. The Red-barred Dragon, for example, will make itself look bigger by erecting the spines along its back, inflating its throat and raising its tail in a coil above the body. This usually causes the intruder to retreat.

The Salt Lake Dragon has adapted to the harsh conditions of the inland salt lakes.

Salt Lake Dragon   17cm

One place where you would not expect to find any reptiles at all is on the salt-encrusted surfaces of dry inland lakes but the small Salt Lake Dragon is found only at Lake Eyre, Lake Torrens and Lake Callabonna in South Australia. Here it burrows into the fine sand beneath the cracked salt crust. It feeds on ants, which live around the edges of the lakes and any other insects that may get blown onto the surface. If the lake floods the dragon is forced by rising waters to leave its shelter and swim to the shore, inflating itself with air in order to remain afloat.

In such a hostile environment this dragon has made a number of adaptations. It has elongated scales at the margin of the lower eyelids that form a prominent fringe and act as a protection from salt glare. It also has a high temperature tolerance and maintains its body temperature at about 30°C.

Chameleon Dragon   35cm

A dragon from northern Australia is almost chameleon-like in its look and habits, and predictably is known as the Chameleon Dragon. It is a tree-dwelling lizard that moves in a very slow, deliberate manner and will freeze when observed. This dragon has a large head and when disturbed it will turn side on and present a laterally flattened body, which gives it the appearance of being larger than it really is. Chameleons are known to behave in a similar manner. Little else is known about this lizard because of its cryptic habits and restricted distribution.

The Chameleon Dragon is a big bluffer.

FOLDS NOT FRILLS

The commonly seen Central Bearded Dragon, which reaches 50 cm in length, and other members of the bearded dragon family are often incorrectly called Frilled Lizards. They do not have a large frill but instead they have folds of skin under their throats. Perching on fence posts and stumps or basking in the middle of roads, these dragons respond to threats by opening their mouths wide and extending these folds to form a beard, thereby presenting a frightening appearance.

How do Reptiles Reproduce?

A female Southern Rainforest Dragon laying eggs on the edge of the forest in a sunny spot.

*T*he majority of reptiles are egg-layers, including all the Australian crocodiles, turtles, blind snakes, pythons, dragons, goannas, geckos and legless lizards. Some egg-layers construct nests; others simply lay them in a secure spot, and still others excavate holes, which they fill in once the eggs are deposited. Common places are in logs, crevices or burrows, or under rocks and other material lying on the ground. Apart from crocodiles, which open the nests and assist the hatchlings to water, and pythons, which coil around their eggs until they incubate, reptile eggs are left by the female and incubate without assistance. A young reptile is on its own from the moment it emerges from the egg.

Are Reptiles' Eggs like Birds' Eggs?

*A*ll snakes' eggs and most other reptilian eggs are leathery or parchment-shelled rather than hard-shelled as in birds. Some gecko eggs are hard-shelled, as are those of the crocodiles and some of the turtles. The softer shells allow the exchange of gases and moisture between the embryo and the outside. If it is too dry, water will be lost from the egg and the embryo will die but too much water will result in the embryo drowning.

Hatchling Lace Monitor. The cutaway shows how tightly packed the fully developed young is within the egg.

Can Temperature Affect Development?

*T*emperature plays an important part in the development of the young reptile inside the egg. Too low a temperature will result in delayed hatching and an increased chance of eggs being found by predators, or the death of the embryos. A one or two degree rise in the incubation temperature can reduce the incubation time considerably. The sex of the hatchlings for some species is also determined by the temperature at which they are incubated. Usually females develop if the temperature is in the higher or lower range, while males result from mid-range temperatures.

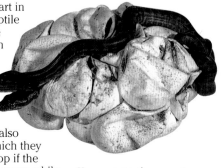

Young carpet pythons emerging from a clutch of eggs.

Why are Some Reptiles Born Alive?

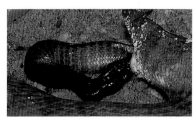

Despite their warm-climate distribution, death adders give birth to live young.

*I*n some species this is an adaptation to living in a cooler climate. In cold regions there are no egg-laying reptiles as laying eggs in these conditions would be very chancy. The cooler soil and air temperatures and the shorter warm seasons would reduce the likelihood of successful incubation. So the female carries the embryos inside her and gives birth to fully developed young.

Can Reptiles Reproduce without Males?

*T*here is a species of blind snake in which the entire population is composed of females. The Flowerpot Snake, so-called because that is where it is often found, occurs in Darwin and arrived by accident from overseas in garden soil. Only one animal was required to established an entire population. By a process known as parthenogenesis, the female can develop a fertile egg without it being fertilised by a male. Several Australian gecko species can also reproduce in this way.

EGG TOOTH

Hatchling reptiles have an egg tooth on their snout. This they use when they are hatching to cut through the shell of the egg with two or three slashes. They will remain in the egg with just the head poking through for up to a day before emerging completely.

Goannas

Tha largest of Australian goannas, a fully grown Perentie is a formidable animal to encounter.

With 26 species occurring here, Australia could really be regarded as the land of the goannas. The word goanna is a corruption of iguana, which is what the early Europeans incorrectly called them; they are more correctly called monitor lizards. Like snakes, goannas have a deeply forked tongue, which is constantly flicked in and out. They are found over most of mainland Australia but the majority of species occur in the northern regions.

Goannas have successfully occupied most habitats and there are several aquatic species, as well as tree-living, rainforest, rock-dwelling and arid-region specialists. They are efficient predators and the larger species are effective scavengers of dead animals. They are also skilled at finding birds' eggs, including those of domestic fowl. The smaller species are mainly insect eaters but they will eat most animals of suitable size.

Huge Ones and Tiny Ones

The largest of the Australian goannas is the Perentie, which can reach 2.5 m in length. Close behind is the Lace Monitor, which can reach 2 m. This species is well known along the east coast and sometimes frequents camping grounds and picnic areas in forested areas. When alarmed it will make for the nearest tree and climb up, keeping the tree trunk between it and the threat.

The smallest of the goannas is the Short-tailed Pygmy Goanna, which only grows to 25 cm. The largest of the pygmy goannas is less than 50 cm in total length. Whether feeding on the ground, in trees or on rocks, pygmy goannas take insects and small lizards; all are extremely wary and quick to seek shelter, which is no wonder as some feature in the diets of larger goannas.

This Sand Goanna is trying to frighten off a threat.

Sand Goanna 1–1.5m

The most widespread of the goannas is the Sand Goanna. This species is found in all mainland States. It invariably has a burrow located within its range to which it retreats if threatened, although it will sometimes climb up a tree. It forages widely and eats a range of prey, including mammals, birds and other reptiles, as well as carrion and birds' and reptiles' eggs. It has been observed digging up the nests of Freshwater Crocodiles to eat their eggs.

The Sand Goanna runs very fast and can do so on two or four legs. When threatened it may stand on two legs and hiss loudly but usually it will run quickly to its burrow. If it cannot reach the burrow it sometimes adopts the strategy of running, then dropping quickly into grass or other vegetation and remaining still. Female Sand Goannas lay up to 11 eggs, which take almost a year to hatch.

The Lace Monitor lays its eggs in termite mounds.

Termite Mound Goannas

Several species of goanna, including the Lace Monitor, use termite nests in which to lay and incubate their eggs. The female will dig through the hard outer shell of the nest and down into the centre. The eggs are laid there and the hole partly filled in. The termites repair the damaged nest within a few days and seal in the eggs. The female remains nearby, presumably to protect the eggs from predators before they are sealed in. The temperature in the nest is constant at about 30°C and the humidity is high. Safe from predation the eggs can incubate under ideal conditions. It appears that the young hatch but remain in the termite nest until they are released by another female digging in to lay her eggs.

THE GOOD OIL

Folklore has it that goanna oil had almost magical properties. Apart from seeping through glass it was purported to cure almost all known complaints. While it makes a good story that's all it is — a story.

81

How Can I Photograph Reptiles?

*R*eptiles as a group are not easy animals to photograph, particularly the lizards and snakes. Rarely do they sit out in the open in an ideal spot for a good photo. Indeed reptiles are more usually under a rock or a piece of tin, in deep shade beneath a shrub or half hidden in a clump of grass. Even when their position is suitable for a shot, they are unlikely to stay there for the time it takes to get the camera organised: no sooner have you started to move in closer for the perfect shot than they run away.

What you Need to Know First

Before attempting serious reptile photography you need to get some understanding about reptiles and their behaviour. So it is worth spending time getting familiar with these animals before undertaking any photography.

Reptile photography usually involves some manipulation of the animal, perhaps positioning it in a more suitable spot, restraining or catching it. As reptiles are protected in all States you must talk to your local wildlife authorities if you intend to do serious reptile photography rather than the snapshot variety. You can normally get permission to disturb reptiles for photographic purposes.

It helps to have someone handle the snake while you photograph it. Below: a photographer observes an Eastern Brown Snake.

Does Photography Stress Reptiles?

*I*n photographing reptiles remember you are dealing with wild animals that are easily stressed. Even if an animal seems quiet and composed, it could be in a state of shock. The result of undue stress could be the death of the animal, either directly or from predation. It could also manifest itself in an unwillingness to feed or to breed, all of which have adverse consequences.

The welfare of the animal is the first consideration and care must be taken not to stress the subject too much. Many reptiles will assume a defensive display when confronted by the camera. If the reptile is in the sun watch that it does not overheat. If a hibernating reptile is found it will be very slow and sluggish. You must make sure it is safely back under cover after the photographs are taken and not just left in the open.

What Equipment Should I Use?

*W*hat photographic equipment you use depends very much on how much you want to spend, whether you want prints or slides, and just how serious you intend to get about photographing reptiles. Professional photographers usually use SLR (single lens reflex) 35 mm cameras with various lenses including a macro or zoom but even with excellent equipment and the technical knowledge, there is no guarantee that you will get excellent pictures every time. You can take good pictures with inexpensive equipment. The most important thing is to almost fill the frame with the subject, use the right exposure and have the subject in focus.

An SLR camera is the best type to get professional shots.

How Many Shots Should I Take?

*O*ne question many people ask is how many photographs should be taken of a subject. It is certainly not unusual to take 10–12 shots to get one good one. Some photographers will take 20 plus. Remember, until the film is developed you will not know if it is a natural-looking or an awkward pose. So several shots provides the opportunity to select the best. When deciding how many to take, ask yourself how easy will it be to photograph this animal again.

What are Skinks?

*T*here are over 300 species of skinks in Australia and it is difficult to generalise on the features of this group of reptiles. They range in size from a few centimetres to over 60 cm and they come in many forms. Most have smooth shiny scales and a long tail that can be cast off easily. Others have a rough prickly skin. Although four limbs are usual, there are species with only two limbs and still others that are completely limbless.

The Blotched Bluetongue is a large skink.

Why do Reptiles Shed their Skins?

*A*ll reptiles have the facility to discard their outer skin. This is known as sloughing or ecdysis. In many snakes this may occur in one piece. Geckos and legless lizards will also shed their skin largely intact but other reptiles do it in a piecemeal manner. Goannas, for example, are sometimes seen with pieces of loose, dead skin hanging off their bodies.

SKIN PROBLEMS

Bluetongues sometimes have a problem with ridding themselves of old skin around their digits. In some cases the old skin dries and hardens, cutting off their blood circulation and thereby causing the loss of all or part of their digit. It is not uncommon to find adult bluetongues with just stumps remaining.

This bluetongue lost its toes from skin shedding.

The outer layer of reptile skin is made up of a material called keratin, which is similar to our finger- or toe-nails; it is keratin that forms a reptile's scales. Scales in reptiles are joined by thinner material and form a continuous layer. (Fish scales on the other hand are separate.) The outer layer of scales suffers a lot of wear and tear as the reptile goes about its normal activities. Because of its composition it cannot expand indefinitely to cope with normal growth. Therefore it is discarded. A new layer of scales form beneath the old one and when this is complete the actual shedding process begins.

Skin shedding occurs more frequently in young reptiles but it does continue throughout life. There is no set time when shedding happens but it usually occurs several times each year.

How Do Snakes 'Peel' Off their Skin?

*T*he first real indication that a snake is about to slough off its skin occurs when the old skin becomes opaque or milky. In snakes this is particularly obvious on the eyes. This is caused by the secretion of an oily fluid between the old and new layers. Snakes are very vulnerable at this time as they have almost no vision. This opaque appearance disappears after a few days and the reptile

A young copperhead snake beginning to shed its skin.

is then ready to commence the process of actually discarding the old skin.

To start the peeling back of its skin, a snake rubs its snout against some rough material, such as rock or bark. Once this starts the snake literally slides out of the old skin, which is left inside out, complete with eye shields.

How Do Lizards Discard their Skin?

*I*n most lizards the skin comes off in bits and many lizards simply slide through litter or grass to assist the process. Geckos shed their skins almost in one piece and they have been observed to eat the old skin. In goannas it comes off in untidy bits and pieces that peel off as the animal moves through grasses and low shrubs.

A Tessellated Gecko in the process of peeling off the old skin. It will come off in almost one piece.

Bluetongue Lizards

15–55 cm

*B*luetongue lizards occur throughout most of Australia and there are five species. So named because of their large deep blue tongues, they are familiar to most people and still manage to survive in suburban gardens. Most of the species will eat just about anything, from snails, slugs, insects and fruit to the food put out for the cat or dog. Although most people like them around the garden because of their snail- and insect-eating abilities, they suffer from the use of snail baits. If they take snails that have eaten snail bait, they will themselves die. Bluetongue lizards produce live young, usually about 10 in a litter but as many as 25 have been recorded.

This Western Bluetongue Lizard is found in semi-arid regions.

Unusual Pygmy Bluetongues

The most unusual of the bluetongues is the Adelaide Pygmy Bluetongue, which is only 15 cm long. It has a very restricted range in South Australia and was thought to be extinct as none had been seen since 1959. However one was found in the stomach of a brown snake in 1992 and several small colonies have since been located. They are very secretive and live in spider burrows, to which they quickly withdraw when disturbed.

The Blotched Bluetongue is the most cold-adapted of the bluetongue lizards and it is found in Tasmania, Victoria and the highlands of southern and central New South Wales. It is also the most colourful with large yellow, pink or orange blotches on the back, although the more southerly populations have only cream or brown blotches.

The rare Adelaide Pygmy Bluetongue.

A colony of Gidgee Skinks bask in the sun.

Arid-region Skinks

The skinks of the arid regions of Australia are numerous and well adapted to living in what can be a very harsh environment. Many have only two or no limbs and spend their time burrowing in the loose sand or litter just beneath the surface. Indeed some that have all four limbs also prefer to spend a lot of time in the top layers of sand. Others shelter in burrows or in deep rock crevices, which are much cooler than the open ground. Burrows have a surprisingly constant year-round temperature and are more humid.

Well-adapted for life in the crevices of rocky outcrops is the Gidgee Skink, a solid, flattened skink. It has short spines on most of its scales and these become very pronounced on its tail. When attacked by a predator, it can jam itself so tightly into a crevice that it is almost impossible to remove.

Comb-eared skinks can be identified by their ear lobes.

Comb-eared Skinks

The 80 or so species of comb-eared skinks are very common in the arid regions of Australia. They are so-called because of the conspicuously enlarged scales or lobes at the front of their ears. These skinks shelter in grasses, in litter or in shallow self-made burrows. Several species may live in the same location but while some are active in the early morning, others do not appear until mid-morning or noon. In this way the different species do not compete directly with one another for the same food. Most of these skinks have bodies patterned with stripes or rows of spots or blotches. Many of these patterns look similar so individual species can be quite difficult to identify.

ESCAPE TUNNELS

The Desert Skink digs a complex system of burrows in which it shelters. Often more than 1.5 m long and consisting of one entrance with a main burrow, there are several side tunnels that stop just below the surface. If a predator starts digging up the burrow the lizard breaks through to the surface from one of its side burrows and escapes.

Rainforest Skinks

At a length of 60 cm, the shy forest-dwelling Land Mullet is Australia's largest skink.

There are some skinks that live only in rainforests. All of them like the high humidity of a rainforest environment and they are intolerant of dry conditions. Several of the burrowing skinks utilise rainforests to burrow beneath logs into the loose soil and mulch. Most rainforest skinks have little need for direct sunlight and are happy to bask in dappled sunlight.

Some Representatives

The Prickly Forest Skink (see map) is a strange little lizard that lives only in the rainforests of northern Queensland. It always seems to pick the coolest and wettest areas and shelters in very damp, waterlogged spots in and under rotting logs, rocks or in holes in banks. It is secretive and rarely seen by day but it is apparently more active at night when it forages for food. It is appears to be very heat sensitive and avoids direct sunlight.

Two other rainforest skinks are the Blue-speckled Forest Skink and the Orange-speckled Forest Skink. These lizards are active during the day and at dusk, and can be seen basking in dappled sunlight in the forest. They are very territorial, although juveniles are tolerated.

There are some skinks that occupy the edges of the rainforest: one of these is the Land Mullet. A giant among skinks, this shiny black, bulky 60-cm lizard slides through the litter of the forest floor in a very imposing way. Although it likes to bask in the sun it is quite wary and never strays very far from cover. While adults are jet black, the young are prettily flecked with bluish white spots.

Pink-tongued Skink

30–45cm

Juvenile Pink-tongued Skink with prominent cross-bands. Inset: these become less distinct with age.

Not many skinks are tree-dwellers but several are partly so. The large Pink-tongued Skink, which lives in moister forest habitats, sometimes at the edges of rainforest, is one that spends some time in trees. It has a long flexible tail, which is ideal for grasping branches as it clambers about on tree limbs and a slender body with remarkably sharp claws. This is a snail and slug eater that hunts at night.

RECENT DISCOVERY
In 1992 a new species of skink was found in Nangur State Forest 250 km northwest of Brisbane. It is a secretive, spiny-scaled skink measuring about 18 cm. So far only found in two areas of vine forest, it lives in burrows. That such a distinctive lizard could remain undiscovered for so long in an area that has been used extensively is surprising.

Colour Changes with Age

This skink produces live young, usually about 15 to 20, although as many as 67 have been recorded. The young are prominently marked with numerous sharp-edged dark cross-bands on the body and tail, which become less distinct as the lizard grows. Some adults lose the bands completely. When the young are born they have bright blue tongues just like a bluetongue lizard's but the colour changes to pink one to two years later, although occasionally adults will be found that still retain the blue tongue.

89

Can I Keep Reptiles?

*B*efore even thinking of obtaining a reptile as a pet you need to consider several points. In all States and Territories of Australia reptiles are protected. You will need to check with your local fauna authorities on what licences are needed. In some States you can only obtain a reptile by transfer from a licensed keeper but in others you can buy them from pet shops.

Bluetongue lizards are popular with reptile keepers.

Reptile-keeping Requirements

It is important to learn about the requirements of the reptile you intend to keep before acquiring one. Caging, lighting, heating and food requirements are the basics that must be set up prior to bringing it home. These will vary depending on whether you have a juvenile or an adult. Some reptiles have very specific require-ments, so you need to be aware of these. Your reptile will be dependent on you for everything and you will be responsible for its health and wellbeing.

It would be a good idea to join the nearest reptile-keeping group. Here you will meet people who share similar interests and most of these groups put out informative news-letters, have regular meet-ings with guest speakers, and can often supply books and equipment at good prices to members.

The licence required to keep reptiles in New South Wales.

NATIONAL PARKS & WILDLIFE ACT, 1974
SECTION 120

FAUNA KEEPERS' LICENCE

Licence Type: **Reptile Keepers' Licence**

Licence Number: **RK 50001**   Licence Class: **2 - Category 2**

Name and Postal Address of Licensee   Nominated Premises

Mr Gerald Swan   94 Yarrabung Rd
94 Yarrabung Rd   ST IVES
ST IVES   NSW 2075
NSW 2075

Date of Issue: **29-Oct-1997**   Expiry Date: **30-Nov-1998**   Signature of Authorised Officer

This licence authorises the person named above to possess, dispose of and obtain protected fauna of the species approved by the NSW National Parks and Wildlife Service ("the Service") to be held under a licence of the type, class and category (if any) shown above. (A copy of the approved species list published by the Service is attached.) This licence is issued subject to the provisions of the National Parks and Wildlife Act, 1974, the regulations thereunder, the general conditions listed below and any special conditions as may be notified in writing to the licensee by the Director-General of National Parks and Wildlife ("the Director-General") or an authorised officer of the Service.

GENERAL CONDITIONS

1. This licence authorises possession of protected fauna at the nominated premises shown above. Where the protected fauna, the subject of this licence, are moved from the nominated premises for any purpose other than disposal/sale or veterinary treatment, the licensee shall forward in writing within seven days to the Director-General, notification of the address of the premises at which the fauna are held.

2. The licensee shall acquire protected fauna of species which may be held under this licence only from a person who is the holder of a current licence issued by the Service which authorises the possession and disposal of those fauna, or from an appropriately licensed person interstate via an Interstate Import Licence issued by the Service, or in any other case only with the prior written consent of the Director-General.

3. Receipt of all protected fauna must be supported by documentary evidence to verify its lawful acquisition, and such evidence must be made available for inspection upon the request of an officer of the Service.

4. The licensee shall dispose of protected fauna which are held under this licence only to a person who is the holder of a current licence issued by the Service which authorises the possession of those fauna, or to an appropriately licensed person interstate via an Export Licence issued by the Service, or in any other case only with the prior written consent of the Director-General.

5. The licensee shall keep at the nominated premises, a true and accurate record in the Fauna Record Book supplied, for each of the holder's acquisitions (including fauna bred - see below) and disposals (including death and escape) of protected fauna. The record shall be completed in accordance with the instructions contained in the Fauna Record Book. The holder shall make the record immediately following each acquisition or disposal. In the case of fauna bred by the licensee, the record is to be completed as follows - reptiles within seven days of birth or hatching as the case may be; amphibians within seven days of resorption of a tadpole's tail; and mammals within seven days of the young being born.

6. The certificate holder shall present the record referred to in Condition 5 to the Director-General or any officer of the Service whenever required. Each completed page of the record shall be signed and dated by the licensee, and shall be forwarded to the Director-General during April each year in the case of reptiles and in August each year in the case of amphibians and mammals.

7. A Licensee who acquires or disposes of species listed in Class 3 of the NSW Reptile or Amphibian Keepers' Licensing Systems must notify the Director-General, in writing within fourteen days of the transaction taking place, of the details of the transaction and the total number of that species held after the transaction.

8. The licensee shall not advertise, except in a publication of an animal keepers' society of which the licensee is a member, for the disposal or acquisition of protected fauna the subject of this licence.

9. The licensee shall not dispose of protected fauna within a period of six months from the date of its acquisition. This condition does not apply to fauna bred by the licensee.

10. All protected fauna shall be housed in escape-proof enclosures and in a manner so as not to be of any danger to the public. Dangerous venomous reptiles may be held only in accordance with the conditions and instructions contained in the NSW National Parks and Wildlife Service pamphlet titled "Reptile Keepers' Licence".

11. The licensee will permit the inspection by an authorised officer of the Service of all fauna held and holding facilities for the purpose of enforcing the provisions of the National Parks and Wildlife Act and the conditions of this licence.

12. The nominated premises must at all times comply with applicable statutory provisions relating to building and health requirements.

Records, notifications and enquiries should be forwarded/directed to:

The Director-General   Phone: 02 9585 6406 or 02 9585 6407
National Parks and Wildlife Service   Fax: 02 9585 6401
PO Box 1967
Hurstville   NSW   2220

How Do I Buy a Reptile?

*I*f you are buying from a shop and know nothing about reptiles ask someone who does to accompany you. While most shops keep their animals in good health, some do not and you could pay a lot of money for a sick or diseased animal of unknown origin.

Eastern Long-necked Turtles make good pets.

Transfers from another keeper, on the other hand, are usually less risky. The reptile you get will be one the keeper has either bred in captivity or kept in captivity for some time. This reduces stress and the likelihood of disease or parasites.

Read John Weigel's book *Care of Australian Reptiles in Captivity* thoroughly and follow the husbandry and caging suggestions. While it does not cover every reptile in Australia, it provides enough information on keeping those that are commonly available to make it an essential item for every reptile keeper.

Reptiles make ideal companion animals for many but they are not affectionate in the same manner as cats or dogs, nor do they become domesticated. They do become used to people and are interesting animals to keep.

Can Pet Reptiles be Kept Inside?

Reptiles can be enjoyable pets.

*I*n many ways reptiles are suitable for high- and medium-density living because most can be kept indoors: they do not take up much space and they do not require daily exercise or feeding. So you can go away for the weekend and leave the lighting and heating on a time switch with a thermostat. Food, be it rats, mice, crickets, meal worms or proprietory brands of reptile food, is readily available from pet shops or other suppliers; your reptile-keeping group may be helpful here.

> **START WITH THE LOCALS**
> It is a good idea to start off with keeping a species that is found in your area. In this way you will have some idea of the animal's requirements, particularly those concerning temperature.

Rock-dwelling Skinks

Cunningham's Skink makes good use of rock crevices. Inset: The Black Mountain Skink lives among black granite boulders.

Many skinks will shelter or forage among rock outcrops but Cunningham's Skink lives in this habitat all the time and it does so very successfully. Distributed down the east coast and across to South Australia, it is a large, robust, easily recognisable lizard with spiny scales. This species is active during the day and occurs in family groups: it is quite possible to see three or four of these lizards basking together on a rock ledge. Flowers and other vegetation form a significant part of their diet.

Restricted Distributions

On Pedra Branca, a sandstone rock off the southern coast of Tasmania, lives the Pedra Branca Skink. This skink has the most southerly distribution of any Australian reptile and an extremely limited range. There is no vegetation to speak of on the rock. The skinks feed on fish scraps and the food regurgitated by seabirds that nest there. In the prevailing cool conditions they will bask in groups to raise their body temperature.

Another rock lizard, which is only known from one area, is the Black Mountain Skink. This lizard only occurs among the black granite boulders at Black Mountain south of Cooktown in Queensland and appropriately it is black to dark brown in colour. It forages during mid-morning and in the late afternoon when the temperature on the rock surfaces is not too hot.

High-altitude Skinks

30–45cm

The Alpine Water Skink makes the most of the short warm season in high-altitude regions. Inset: a Tussock Cool Skink.

The sub-alpine and alpine habitats are not usually thought of as being ideal areas for reptiles but there are some skinks that occupy these regions very successfully. The Alpine Water Skink, the Tussock Cool Skink and the Tasmanian Snow Skink are some that live in high-altitude areas. The Tussock Cool Skink is found from the coast to the top of Mount Kosciuszko and has the greatest altitude range of any Australian reptile (see map).

Adaptations to the High Life

In summer the number of skinks seen in alpine meadows is very noticeable but to survive winter these skinks must hibernate deep in the soil or within large rotten logs.

The majority of alpine skinks give birth to live young because egg development is slow in these low temperatures and young may hatch too late in the season to survive winter. Some alpine skinks mate in autumn with the female storing sperm over winter. When they emerge from hibernation in spring they can concentrate on feeding rather than mating activities. Breeding every second year is another strategy employed by several alpine skinks. A further adaptation to life in the high country is displayed by some Tasmanian species, which have a tinted 'window' in their lower eyelids, presumably a reptilian equivalent to our sunglasses, serving to reduce glare.

Checklist of Australian Reptiles

The following is a list of the most common and best known snakes and other reptiles in Australia. There are many other more obscure reptiles, especially among the geckos and skinks.

Common Name (Family)	Genus

SNAKES

Colubrids (Colubridae)

Brown Tree Snakes	*Boiga*
Green Tree Snakes	*Dendrelaphis*
Freshwater Snakes	*Tropidonophis*
White-bellied Mangrove Snake	*Fordonia*

Elapids (Elapidae)

Death Adders	*Acanthophis*
Rough-scaled Snakes	*Tropidechis*
Bardicks	*Echiopsis*
Tiger Snakes	*Notechis*
Southern Snakes	*Drysdalia*
Copperheads	*Austrelaps*
Taipans	*Oxyuranus*
Brown Snakes	*Pseudonaja*
Black Snakes	*Pseudechis*
Whipsnakes	*Demansia*
Crowned Snakes	*Cacophis*
Bandy Bandys	*Vermicella*
Other Elapids	*Hoplocephalus*
	Rhinoplocephalus
	Suta
	Furina

Blind Snakes (Typhlopidae)	*Ramphotyphlops*
File Snakes (Acrochordidae)	*Acrochordus*
Pythons (Boidae)	*Aspidites*
	Liasis
	Morelia
	Antaresia

TURTLES
Sea Turtles (Cheloniidae, Dermochelyidae)
Freshwater Turtles (Carettochelydidae, Chelidae)

CROCODILES (Crocodylidae)   *Crocodylus*

LIZARDS

Geckos (Gekkonidae)
  Clawless Geckos   *Crenadactylus*
  Dtellas   *Gehyra*
  Prickly Geckos   *Heteronotia*
  Knob Tail Geckos   *Nephrurus*
  Velvet Geckos   *Oedura*
  Leaf Tails   *Phyllurus*
  Ring-tailed Gecko   *Cyrtodactylus*
  Other Geckos   *Pseudothecadactylus*
                                  Diplodactylus

Dragons (Agamidae)
  Frilled Lizard   *Chlamydosaurus*
  Bearded Dragons   *Pogona*
  Forest Dragons   *Hypsilurus*
  Water Dragons   *Physignathus*
  Thorny Devil   *Moloch*
  Chameleon Dragon   *Chelosania*
  Lashtails   *Amphibolurus*
  Two-line Dragons   *Diporiphora*
  Other Dragons   *Ctenophorus*
                                  Tympanocryptis

Legless Lizards (Pygopodidae)
  Burton's Legless Lizard   *Lialis*
  Worm Lizards   *Aprasia*
  Scaly-foots   *Pygopus*

Goannas (Varanidae)   *Varanus*

Skinks (Scincidae)
  Bluetongues   *Tiliqua*
  Shinglebacks   *Trachydosaurus*
  Sliders   *Lerista*
  Prickly Forest Skink   *Gnypetoscincus*
  Rainbow Skinks   *Carlia*
  Sand Swimmers   *Eremiascincus*
  Worm Skinks   *Anomalopus*
  Comb-eared Skinks   *Ctenotus*
  Slender Bluetongues   *Cyclodomorphus*
  Pink-tongued Skink   *Hemisphaeriodon*
  Other Skinks   *Cryptoblepharus*
                                  Egernia
                                  Eulamprus
                                  Lampropholis
                                  Pseudemoia
                                  Nangura
                                  Niveoscincus

INDEX